FINAL FLIGHT

Volume I

John Evans

Published by:
PATERCHURCH PUBLICATIONS,
6 Laws Street, Pembroke Dock, SA72 6DL
Tel: 01646 683041
www.paterchurch-publications.co.uk

Designed and printed by Haven Colourprint UK, Pembroke Dock

First printed: October 2005   © *John Evans 2005*

ISBN: 1 870745 14 0

ACCIDENT LOCATIONS

FOREWORD

I could so easily have been on Liberator EV881 when it crashed in the Preseli Hills in September 1944. By one of those quirks of fate I missed joining my crew for what should have been just another training flight.

Arriving at the runway, I remember seeing the Liberator take off on what was its last journey. Although it was not my fault I still feel guilty to have missed the final flight.

I have often thought about the accident and the fate of my crew - we had carried out six operational missions and seven training flights together. Then, in 1984, I was contacted by the Pembrokeshire Aviation Group and was so pleased to be able to join the commemoration to mark the 40th anniversary of the accident.

Since then I have had the pleasure of returning to Pembrokeshire on several occasions to attend events linked to EV881 anniversaries.

I have known John Evans ever since my first visit. He is very dedicated and committed to the cause of aviation history and I am so pleased that he has, at last, written about Liberator EV881's final flight and of Stan Kearey and his fine crew.

It is good to know that John has also recorded other aviation incidents which have a connection with west Wales. Several of these, as with EV881, ended in tragic circumstances. The stories of these are now on record and the sacrifices of the airmen involved shall always be remembered.

Danny Quinn, BEM
BOULOGNE SUR MER, France.
September 2005

Sergeant Danny Quinn, No 547 Squadron, RAF, in 1945

CHAPTER I

Great War seaplane in harbour crash
Sopwith Baby seaplane N1033, April 22nd 1917

Taking the waters... A Sopwith Baby in its element. Its single Lewis gun can just be seen above the upper wing. *Donald Hannah Collection via MAP*

Officers... Four Royal Navy Air Service officers are pictured by a beached Sopwith Baby at Fishguard. Flight Lieutenant R. E. Bush is known to be in the group, along with Flight Sub Lieutenants W. G. Westcott, H. F. Delarue and R. G. Clarke. The aircraft is almost certainly N1033 which Flight Lieutenant Bush was flying on April 22nd 1917. *Ken Williams Collection*

For those who know where to look at Fishguard Harbour, a black scar on a cliff-face is a sad and lasting reminder of one of the earliest aviation accidents in Pembrokeshire - one which claimed the life of a young pilot in the Great War.

Early in 1917 work began to create a seaplane station at the North Pembrokeshire port. This was one of many air stations set up around the British coastline to counter the menace of the German submarines.

Throughout the First World War German U-boats sank large numbers of merchant vessels and were a major threat to the whole war effort. The operation of airships, seaplanes and land planes on coastal patrols from various UK locations was one element of the defences set up to deter the submarines' activities.

An airship station had already been set up at Milton, near Carew Castle, in 1915 and the establishment of the Royal Naval Air Station at Fishguard brought a second air base into operation in west Wales, to patrol the Irish Sea area.

On the three-acre site, to the north of the railway station at Goodwick, a canvas and wood hangar was quickly erected, along with sheds and a slipway to launch and recover the seaplanes.

One of the first airmen posted to the new station was Flight Lieutenant Richard Eldon Bush, a 26-year-old pilot. On April 22nd 1917 Bush prepared to test a Sopwith Baby seaplane, N1033, following the fitting of a new engine. Surprisingly for what appeared to be just a test flight two 16lb bombs were also carried under the wings of the stubby biplane.

Bush took off from the harbour but failed to gain enough height to clear power cables linking the power house with the wireless station. The aircraft's twin floats caught the cables and the seaplane crashed into a cliff face, bursting into flames.

Bravely a sentry, Private B. Blackburn of the King's Liverpool Regiment, rushed to Bush's aid and pulled him from the burning wreckage at the base of the cliff. The two men, and others on the scene, were thankfully some distance from the wreckage when the bombs exploded.

Bush, burned but fully conscious, was taken by ambulance to his quarters at the nearby Bay Hotel - which served as the officers' mess - and was treated there by Dr H. Mortimer Thomas, the Admiralty medical officer. There was every hope that he would make a recovery but his condition suddenly worsened and in the early hours of April 24th he died.

Local newspapers reported in detail on the accident and its aftermath, censorship not being a major constraint for local journalists in the Great War. *The West Wales Guardian* reported a sad postscript, noting: 'One most pathetic circumstance in connection with the demise is that the deceased had written to the vicar, the Rev E. Lincoln Lewis, on Sunday morning last requesting him to call the banns as he intended marrying'.

FATAL FLYING ACCIDENT

TRAGIC SCENE AT GOODWICK.

Young Officer's Sad End.

Last Sunday evening a serious accident occurred to Flight-Lieut. Bush (24), at Fishguard Harbour. With the view of testing the new engine with which the "bus" had been fitted the previous day, Lieut. Bush set out along the Irish quay with the object of rising, head to wind, over the electric power station. Starting off he scudded along increasing speed and got fairly well up when, however, the machine failed to clear the obstacles, the floats hitching on the cables that convey current to the wireless station. The contact caused the 'plane to swerve to port, and it struck the cliff, the compact smashing the machine and, it is believed, the young officer's head also came into contact with the rock. Immediately the petrol caught fire, and in a few moments the 'plane crashed to earth between the contractors' air-compressing shed and the cliff, and burned furiously. Pte. Blackburn, of the King's (Liverpool) Regiment, who was on sentry duty in the vicinity, rushed to the officer's assistance, extricated him, and dragged him away from the flaming mass. With great presence of mind, Lieut. Bush, whose clothes were ablaze, rolled himself on the ground, and succeeded in subduing the fire, though he was burned on the face and hands and left thigh. An ambulance trolly was brought up, and the young aviator was placed thereon still perfectly conscious. The men and ambulance had drawn away several yards when two 16-pound bombs exploded by the heat, happily they did not cause further damage to life and limb. So composed was the young officer that he remarked on hearing the explosion that the bombs had gone off. The air-compressor building was damaged a little by the flames, but not so as to interfere with the machinery.

Lieut Bush was taken to his quarters, the Bay Hotel, and Dr. H. Mortimer Thomas, the Admiralty medical officer, was quickly in attendance upon the sufferer. During the evening and all night Dr. Thomas was in attendance, and from the patient's cheerful condition every hope was entertained that he would recover. On Monday, however, internal hemorrhage set in, and, although he maintained consciousness almost to the end, Lieut. Bush passed away about 5 o'clock on Tuesday morning.

During the brief period he had been at Fishguard the deceased had won much admiration and esteem. Indeed, the officers and men have impressed all most favourably, and the sincerest sympathy is everywhere manifest. One most pathetic circumstance in connection with the demise is that the deceased had written to the vicar, the Rev. E. Lincoln Lewis, on Sunday morning last, requesting him to call the banns as he intended marrying.

Report... How the *West Wales Guardian* reported on Flight Lieutenant Bush's fatal accident.
Author's Collection

Funeral procession... Three views as Flight Lieutenant Bush's coffin was escorted from the Bay Hotel to the nearby railway station. These photographs were taken by Charles Edwards of Fishguard and produced as postcards.

Flight Lieutenant Bush's sorrowing parents, Mr and Mrs Philip Bush, travelled from their home at The Old Manor House, Keynsham, near Bristol, to attend the funeral which was conducted with full military honours. The cortage, escorted by colleagues from RNAS Fishguard, proceeded from the Bay Hotel to Fishguard and Goodwick railway station. From there the coffin was taken home to Bristol. Richard Eldon Bush lies at Keynsham Cemetery.

During a visit to Fishguard and Goodwick made by members of the Pembrokeshire Aviation Group some years ago historian Ken Williams pointed out the site where the Sopwith Baby had crashed. A fire blackened scar could still be made out. When casually looking around the site the Author found a piece of fused metal which may well have come from the seaplane, testifying to the ferocity of the blaze which consumed the aircraft.

* Sopwith Baby N1033 was one of many of the type built by the Blackburn Aircraft Company at Leeds and was powered by a 110 hp Clerget rotary engine. The single-seater Babies were armed with one Lewis machine gun and two bombs and had a top speed of nearly 100 mph. Nearly 300 Sopwith Baby seaplanes were built; one survives and is displayed at the Fleet Air Arm Museum, Yeovilton, Somerset.

** The site where the Sopwith crashed is on private land.

Top: Royal Naval Air Service personnel provided the escort for the flower bedecked coffin as the cortege left the Fishguard Bay Hotel.
Martin Lewis Collection

Middle: With rifles reversed, men of the 3rd Garrison Battalion, The King's Liverpool Regiment, formed a guard of honour at Goodwick Railway Station as the funeral cortege approached. The guard was commanded by Captain R. Shannon of the 15th Worcesters.
Ken Williams Collection

Below: Flight Lieutenant Bush's parents, Mr and Mrs Philip Bush, are seen standing between the two rows of soldiers.
Martin Lewis Collection/Ken Williams Collection

CHAPTER II

Miraculous escape on Carn Ingli
Bellanca NR 13137 'Leonardo da Vinci', August 18th 1934

In rural west Wales in the 1930s the sight and sound of an aeroplane was a rarity and when one did appear it always prompted great interest. For the residents of Newport a stormy summer's night in 1934 brought an aeroplane literally into their community, dropping out of the sky to crash on the slopes of Carn Ingli mountain.

The story behind the unexpected arrival of the single-engined monoplane - and the remarkable survival of its two-man crew - is still remembered today and has become part of the folklore of this north Pembrokeshire community.

Newport residents still awake in the very early hours of Sunday August 18th were surprised to hear the sound of an aircraft flying low. Although high summer it was blowing a gale and raining heavily. Then the sound disappeared.

What could so easily have been a double tragedy turned out instead to be a very lucky escape for two pioneer aviators - an American, Captain George Pond, and his Italian colleague, Lieutenant Cesare Sabelli. Their Bellanca - a high wing monoplane with a powerful 300 hp radial engine - had hit the mountainside and flipped over onto its back.

From the badly damaged aircraft Pond and Sabelli extricated themselves and counted their lucky stars as neither was seriously hurt. Then they set out for help.

Beach attraction... Crowds flocked to Aberavon Beach to see the Leonardo da Vinci after its unscheduled landing on the outward journey to Italy. *Arthur Jones*

What happened next has been recounted by Port Talbot-based historian Arthur Jones, who has researched the last flight of the Bellanca.

"...The two men made their way by torchlight to the nearest farmhouse to seek help but were thought to be tramps and were told 'clear off and shut the gate' and so had to return to the crash site where they spent the night sleeping on the wings of the aircraft.

"Shortly after dawn they walked to another farmhouse where they had better luck and were taken to the Commercial Hotel in Newport. For the next few days they were virtually feted, being invited to dinner at Newport Castle as well as other engagements."

Interest... The Bellanca, battered but remarkably intact, lies on the Carn Ingli hillside, the focal point of much interest. Severe damage to the fixed undercarriage can be seen but the propeller appears virtually intact, apart from a chunk missing near the blade tip on the right.
Both Raymond Lewis

The bright red aircraft, with 'Leonardo da Vinci' prominently painted on its fuselage, soon became a magnet for local residents. People from a wide area trekked up the slopes to view the machine, which was upside down but remarkably intact. Many photographs were taken and remain in local collections along, it is said, with pieces of the machine which were collected as souvenirs.

'Leonardo da Vinci' was later taken to Newport Garage and, it is believed, crated up for shipment, presumably from Fishguard Harbour, back to the United States.

The aircraft had been on a return flight from Rome to the USA. Earlier, in May, it had completed a west-east Atlantic crossing and had made a safe landfall at Aberavon Beach, Port Talbot.

Pond and Sabelli were attempting a record double crossing of the Atlantic from New York to Rome and back. On the outward flight engine trouble had forced them to land on Ireland's west coast, followed by a further stop at Dublin. On the subsequent flight over the Irish Sea engine problems returned and so the aviators made a precautionary landing on the sands of Aberavon.

An engineer was flown down from Cardiff aerodrome - at Pengam Moors - and repairs were made, enabling the two men to fly on and they reached Rome. There they were royally received and met the Italian dictator, Mussolini, who presented them with cigarette cases.

On the return flight on August 18th things went badly wrong. Heading for Dublin, the pilots encountered heavy mist, fog and rain and after flying blind for some time they returned to the Welsh coast and circled, hoping to make a dawn landing. They must have been flying very low as Carn Ingli 'got in the way'.

A *West Wales Guardian* reporter, who interviewed the two airmen just hours after the crash, recorded that Pond had had medical attention for a painful back while Sabelli had bruises to his back and legs. A later X-ray on Pond showed up a dislocated rib. But these were minor injuries - they had had a 'miraculous escape'.

Sabelli told the reporter that having turned back to the Welsh coast all they could see was the light of Strumble Head lighthouse.

"We were circling around at.....1,200 feet, hoping to make a landing at dawn when, without warning, we struck something. The aeroplane rose and after 100 yards struck the ground and turned a somersault. We managed to extricate ourselves and for a time sat by the side of the machine. We were dazed and did not know where we were but congratulated ourselves on our escape."

After the initial rebuff at one farmhouse - callers were not expected at 4 am! - the airmen were given hospitality, as dawn broke, at Blaenffynon Farm, home of the John family. Also in the farmhouse were Mr and Mrs Gwilym Davies visiting from Llanelli. It was Mr Davies who arranged a meal for the airmen before taking them to the hotel.

The *Guardian* reported that hundreds of visitors made the steep climb up to the crash scene on the Sunday afternoon and Monday, the aircraft being watched over by two local men, J. Wilde and F. Humphries.

Lieutenant Sabelli at least stayed on in the locality for several weeks, the *Guardian* reporting in its December 7th edition that he had the previous Sunday morning 'taken his final leave of Newport - not without considerable regret'.

There may have been an anniversary sequel to the Carn Ingli crash story. In late 1984 the Author was informed by a Newport contact that one of the airmen had returned to the area earlier in the summer. By then, of course, the trail had gone cold.

It will never now be known if Pond or Sabelli had, indeed, made a nostalgic visit exactly 50 years on from their sudden arrival from the skies on a dark and stormy night.

Court Leet... During his stay in the Newport area Lieutenant Cesare Sabelli was received by the Newport Court Leet. This photograph was taken outside Commerce House, just round the corner from the Llwyngwair Arms were the Court Leet was held. The names of all in the photograph are known. Lieutenant Sabelli is the smartly suited gent with the bow tie standing next to Lady Lloyd. On her left is the Mayor, Alderman Caleb Morris. *Dillwyn Miles*

CHAPTER III

Gunnery training 'write off'
Wellington I L4232, September 19th 1939

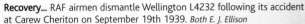

Recovery... RAF airmen dismantle Wellington L4232 following its accident at Carew Cheriton on September 19th 1939. *Both E. J. Ellison*

The first air station for land planes to be established in Pembrokeshire was RAF Carew Cheriton, near to the pretty villages of Milton and Sageston and Carew's famous Norman castle.

In the Great War this had been a naval air station operating airships and was then known as RNAS Pembroke. After the war the land had returned to agricultural use but in 1939, as war clouds loomed over Europe, it was again taken over for a military purpose.

During that spring and summer there was intense activity on the site. The *West Wales Guardian* in an April issue recorded: 'The work has been carried out at a rapid pace and already long lines of huts have been completed. Two large hangars appear to be completed. The station has been manned and in the numerous tents which provide temporary accommodation a big unit of the RAF is already on duty'.

Hawker Henleys of B Flight, No 1 Anti-Aircraft Co-operation Unit, were the first aircraft to arrive, in the April. A single seater with many similarities to its stablemate, the Hurricane, the Henleys were tasked to tow targets which were fired upon by anti-aircraft units stationed around the Welsh coast, including nearby Manorbier, and in air-to-air practice by various types of aircraft.

It was to Carew Cheriton that No 99 Squadron, one of Bomber Command's front line units, sent aircraft in September 1939 for gunnery training. In those early weeks of the war the RAF's bomber force was expected to carry out raids in daylight, in the belief that well armed bombers would always get through to their targets. Early daylight raids were to prove this philosophy painfully wrong and very costly.

Among the 99 Squadron Wellingtons which flew in from their Newmarket base was L4232, a Mark I. On September 19th this aircraft was prepared for another sortie, its crew of six including four gunners on a gunnery training detail.

What happened prior to the crash is not clear as there is confusing information. Some sources say that L4232 collided with Henley L3249 while landing at Carew Cheiton. Yet the Operational Record Book of 99 Squadron, held at the National Archives at Kew, gives another side of the story.

Former 99 Squadron aircrewman Bill Simmonds, who studied the ORB at Kew, wrote to the Author: 'I looked up the official remarks about L4232. The result - words to the effect that a phone call (or signal?) from Carew Cheriton said that L4232 had crashed on take off due to engine failure and had been so badly damaged it was considered a write off. No mention of a Henley aircraft.'

If Henley L3249 was involved it was not seriously damaged as records show that this aircraft soldiered on until crashing in Essex in July 1943.

What is certain is that the Wellington was indeed a write off. In the 1980s former RAF Flight Sergeant E. J. Ellison, then living at Laugharne, loaned the Author a series of superb photographs taken at Carew Cheriton during the first months of its operational use. These included two photos of L4232 after the crash.

The first shot shows the badly damaged aircraft on its belly. The starboard outer wing is missing, having already been dismantled, and the starboard Pegasus radial engine is in the process of being removed.

The other photograph was taken from the starboard side and shows in detail the engine mounting for the Pegasus. The aircraft is likely to have carried the LN code letters allocated to 99 Squadron in September 1939. Certainly it had an individual letter on the side of the fuselage but this letter is not clear from the photograph.

While L4232 never flew again parts recovered from the wreck would have been recycled onto other Wellingtons and the remaining metal used as scrap.

Crew list: Flight Sergeant J. W. Brent, Pilot
Sergeant H. P. Atkinson, Navigator
Leading Aircraftsman S. K. Love
Aircraftsman 1 H. E. Beaumont
Aircraftsman 2 E. H. Wills
Aircraftsman 2 J. W. Haynes

The four aircraftsmen were the gunnery detail. All the crew members were listed as injured.

* Two members of this crew were lost on operations with 99 Squadron. LAC Beaumont was killed on December 14th 1939 when his aircraft was shot down into the sea and Pilot Flight Sergeant Brent died, along with his five crew, when their Wellington crashed into the sea off the English coast in May 1940.

CHAPTER IV

Battles lost
Fairey Battle K7688, February 26th 1940

Batch... A Fairey Battle from the same production batch as the Preseli casualty. This one is K7558 which ended its days in a forced landing in Devon in August 1940. *Richard Lindley*

The Preseli Hills in Pembrokeshire are not high - the tallest point is only 535 metres (1,760 feet) above sea level - but several aircraft have come to grief on these hills, both in wartime and in peacetime.

For well over 60 years substantial parts of a Fairey Battle bomber have remained on a windswept Preseli ridge. Even now, despite the attentions of souvenir hunters, the parts are recognisable as coming from an aeroplane.

The Battle was a single engined, three seat light bomber which was one of the RAF's frontline aircraft at the beginning of the war in September 1939. A monoplane of attractive lines and powered by a Rolls-Royce Merlin engine, it was obsolescent by the outbreak of war but continued in extensive service due to a shortage of more up-to-date types. In the Battle of France in the summer of 1940 the Fairey Battle squadrons paid a very heavy price against German fighters.

All this was to come when Battle K7688, of No 9 Bombing and Gunnery School, RAF Penrhos, near Pwllheli, North Wales, took off on a cross-country flight to Ashton Down in Gloucester on February 26th. It was a bleak winter's day and the crew of pilot Sergeant T. Forbes and Sergeant N. V. Pleno soon ran into low cloud. When a forced landing became inevitable Sergeant Forbes, with considerable skill, brought the aircraft down on the Preseli hillside and both crewmen remarkably walked away unhurt. Their crumpled Battle was left behind to be recovered by a salvage squad.

Aviation author David Smith - who for many years penned a regular 'Wreckovery' column in the *Aviation News* paper - came up with some fascinating information on the subsequent recovery operation.

He was given access to notes made by Mr J. Wilson, a member of No 50 Maintenance Unit based at Cowley, Oxfordshire. Mr Wilson was leader of No 24 Gang of 50 MU which travelled extensively throughout the midlands and south-western parts of Britain in the early war years retrieving wrecked aircraft.

The notes recall the Battle recovery in March 1940.

'Had position of crash pointed out to us by the nearest farmer to the site. Too late to climb the mountain so went to Cardigan for digs. Started on the job next day - March 14th - after crossing three miles of bogland before climbing last peak of mountain.

Roundel... Cadets from No 585 (Milford Haven) Squadron, Air Training Corps, found the substantial remains of a wing from the Fairey Battle when they visited the site in 1982. Part of the RAF roundel could then still be made out, together with yellow and black paint on the undersurface of the wing. Target-towing aircraft were given yellow and black hatching on the undersurfaces to identify them for their mundane but very necessary role. *Author*

'Managed to salvage Merlin engine and instruments. Had to dig hole 30 feet by 16 feet by five feet deep to bury airframe after dismantling and using 140 gallons of petrol to burn it. Worked in rain and cloud most of the time.

'Brought engine back in lorry. Stayed at Abergavenny on way back to Cowley. Hire of horses £4 per journey. Farmer would only go up the mountain twice. Job lasted ten days.'

When the Author first visited the crash site with an ATC squadron in the early 1980s part of a wing was substantially intact. Gradually, over the years, bits of the Battle continued to be 'souvenired'. The RAF roundel which was prominent on the upper surface of the wing was cut out and removed and now just skeletal parts remain, stark reminders of a remarkable feat of airmanship.

What though of the burnt remains buried on site

Bits and pieces... By September 2004 many parts of the Battle had disappeared from the hillside. Pembrokeshire Aviation Group members Dave James (left) and Geraint Pynn examine what was left.
Nick Harris

by Wilson and his team? These must still lie beneath the grass and heather on this bleakly beautiful hillside.

Three casualties

Months before the Preseli crash landing another Fairey Battle was lost in Pembrokeshire, this time in tragic circumstances.

On October 29th 1939 - just a few weeks after war had been declared - the three crew of Battle K9472 were killed when the aircraft crashed near RAF Station Carew Cheriton.

The aircraft and crew were from No 35 Squadron - at that time a training unit based at Cranfield in Bedfordshire - which two days earlier had detached four Battles with pilots and eight air gunners to Carew Cheriton for air gunnery training. The aircraft was seen to be in trouble and circling and may have

been on fire before it crashed. It came down close to the tidal mill which is near Carew Castle.

Ministry of Defence records state that the Battle was on an air firing practice. 'It turned cross wind just after take off, then turned left downwind towards the airfield. The aircraft lost height and flew into cliff face'.

K9472's crew was: Pilot Officer Geoffrey Arthur Cyril Rhind, Aircraftsman 1 Ewart Wynne Looker and Aircraftsman 2 Bernard Connor. Rhind, who was buried at Abingdon, is listed in the Commonwealth War Graves Commission records as a Pilot Officer but other sources give his rank as Flying Officer. Twenty-year-old Looker was taken for burial at Prestatyn's Coed Bell Cemetery while Connor was interred at St Kentigern's Roman Catholic Cemetery, Glasgow.

*Grid reference for the site of Battle K7688 is SN 127325.

CHAPTER V

Ansons accidents

Avro Ansons K6285 and N9742, 1940

Close company... One of the series of photographs taken over west Wales countryside with Anson K6285 leading N9742. Although it cannot be easily seen on this particular photograph the code letters MW can still be made out on K6285 - a legacy of its time on the strength of 217 Squadron, RAF, which operated a detachment at Carew Cheriton. This coding has, over the years, confused aviation writers. K6285 was with 321 Squadron when it was photographed and when it made its last flight. The sloping windscreen, a characteristic of the very early Ansons, can be seen to good effect on K6285 as distinct from the more angular version on N9742 and the majority of others Mark Is. *Royal Netherlands Naval Air Service*

The German Blitzkrieg through France, Belgium and The Netherlands in 1940 brought a new word into the English language, shattered the so-called 'Phoney War' and led directly to establishing a link between Pembrokeshire and the Dutch nation which endured for 65 years.

In May 1940, following the German invasion of neutral Netherlands, many Dutch servicemen escaped to Britain to continue the fight. Among them were Dutch Navy personnel with their Fokker T-VIII-W twin-engined floatplanes. The hard-pressed RAF soon found a role for the modern Dutch seaplanes and they were sent post-haste to RAF Station Pembroke Dock to form up as a RAF unit.

Two squadrons formed at Pembroke Dock at the beginning of June 1940 from the nucleus of escaping Dutch personnel, the numbers 320 and 321 being allocated to the new units.

For No 320 Squadron, operating the Fokker floatplanes, 'PD' was to be home for the next few months, the attractive looking monoplanes, now camouflaged and with RAF roundels, operating in support of the Sunderland flying-boats.

There was enough personnel to form No 321 Squadron, but not enough aircraft, so the RAF despatched the new unit a few miles eastward to RAF Carew Cheriton. Here the squadron was allocated the first of a familiar and well respected type, the Avro Anson.

As the summer of 1940 turned to autumn, and the Battle of Britain made headlines, 321 Squadron quietly went about its new tasks, training up its crews, assisted by RAF personnel, and taking its turn in convoy protection patrols over coastal waters.

That summer a series of photographs of Ansons from the Dutch unit was taken, the field patterns of west Wales forming a peaceful and timeless backdrop.

The photographs centred on Ansons K6285 and N9742. They both had standard RAF camouflage and roundels but also proudly carried a unique marker - an inverted orange triangle, with black edging - to signify their Dutch connections. The triangles were painted on the fins of these particular Ansons but

featured on the forward fuselages of others of the type operated by the squadron.

Before the end of a very dramatic year both photocall Ansons had been lost in accidents, happily without major casualties.

For K6285 - one of the first production batch of Ansons characterised by a distinctive sloping windscreen - its final flight came in the early hours of August 9th. Dutch pilot Sergeant J. P. J. Bielfeldt had taken off on a training flight shortly after midnight but became lost and attempted a forced landing on Pendine Sands.

Pendine's famous sands - the centre for speed record attempts pre-war - were not the wide open spaces of peacetime days. Fear of invasion had led to British beaches being festooned with anti-invasion obstacles and the Anson hit one of these and came down heavily in the sea. Happily, Bielfeldt - thought to be the only one on board - reached shore safely.

The following day work began to recover the Anson. Although too badly damaged to be repaired to flying condition K6285 was destined for another role - as an instructional airframe with the maintenance number 2398M. Its final fate is not recorded but ultimately it would have been scrapped.

N9742's last flight was an operational convoy protection patrol on 29th November. Sergeant Pilot C. I. Van Kooy and his three crew were forced to ditch in the sea off Holyhead, Anglesey, following an engine failure. The aircraft sank and van Kooy's crew colleagues - whose names are not known - were

Archibald Willis, the 20-year-old RAF airman who lost his life when Anson K8829 crashed on July 31st 1940. He lies in the beautifully kept War Graves section of Carew Cheriton Cemetery. *Deric Brock Collection*

Archibald Willis, who was just 20, was buried at Carew Cheriton Cemetery while Sergeant Tomley was taken to Seaford, Sussex, for burial.

Almost exactly 50 years later, during the weekend of the Third Flying-Boat Reunion at Pembroke Dock, Dutch veteran Johannes van der Schaaf returned to Carew Cheriton and the village cemetery where he paid his respects to Archibald Willis, his young crew colleague from Anson K8829.

Two other Carew Cheriton Ansons were lost in 1940, this time through a Luftwaffe raid on the airfield. In the early morning attack, on October 1st, K6175 and K8823 - both from the first production batch - were destroyed on the ground.

reported to be injured. It is likely that the Anson was still carrying the individual code letter Y as seen when it was photographed.

These were not the only Anson losses involving Dutch personnel from Carew Cheriton. On July 31st 1940 three Dutch airmen and two RAF men prepared to take off in K8829, an aircraft on charge to 48 Squadron but assigned to the Royal Netherlands Naval Air Service.

As it made its take off run the Anson hit a dispersed Battle, N2050, and burst into flames. The three Dutchmen, Sergeant A. J. Daniels, Lieutenant Commander Kolff and Corporal J. van der Schaaf, were injured. Tragically, their RAF colleagues, Flight Sergeant S. P. Tomley and Sergeant A. G. Willis, were killed.

Fifty years on... Dutch veterans Johannes van der Schaaf (right) - who survived the crash of Anson K8829 - and Arnold Geudeker, who served in Pembrokeshire in the early days of Nos 320 and 321 Squadrons, were among the Dutch party who attended the Third Flying-Boat Reunion in Pembroke Dock in 1990. They are pictured with Betty Parsons, Pembroke Dock Theme Week's 'Miss 1930s'. *Author*

The final chapter in the links between the squadrons and the communities of Pembroke Dock and Carew - begun in wartime and re-established in the 1980s during the sequence of Flying-Boat Reunions - was written in January 2005. Just days before Nos 320 and 321 Squadrons of the Royal Netherlands Navy disbanded at their home base of Valkenburg, representatives of both units visited Pembrokeshire. They brought with them two magnificent plaques of the crests of the squadrons, for display at the Gun Tower Museum in Pembroke Dock, and a unique piece of artwork, depicting the history of the two squadrons, which was presented to the Carew Cheriton Control Tower Committee.

During the visit the Dutch party also paid their own tributes to the six Netherlands airmen who are buried at Carew Cheriton and Pembroke Dock's Llanion cemeteries.

Top: Museum gifts... The two magnificent plaques of the crests of 320 and 321 Squadrons were presented at the Pembroke Dock Town Council Chamber in January 2005. Pictured, left to right: Councillor John Thomas, Chairman of Pembrokeshire County Council; Commander Arie Louter, CO of 321 Squadron; John Evans, Pembroke Dock Museum Trust; Commander Marc de Jong, CO of 320 Squadron; Councillor Ron Watts, Deputy Mayor and Honorary Curator of the Gun Tower Museum, and Councillor Don Esmond, Mayor of Pembroke Dock. The plaques went on display at the town's Gun Tower Museum for the 2005 season. *Martin Cavaney Photography*

Bottom: Control Tower... Deric Brook, Chairman of the Carew Cheriton Control Tower Committee, received the unique artwork from Commander Arie Louter (left) and Commander Marc de Jong. *Martin Cavaney Photography*

CHAPTER VI

Disaster on town's doorstep
Vickers Wellington Ic N2749, July 19th 1942

Wimpey... Identical examples to Wellington Ic N2749 are seen in this photograph. Affectionately known as the 'Wimpey', the type gave sterling service throughout World War II and was still in use as a trainer in the 1950s. *Imperial War Museum CH720*

● Mr Tom Martin points to where the Wellington bomber crashed.

Riddle of bomber crash-site solved

Location... A cutting from the *Western Mail* of March 1986 with Mr Tom Martin pointing out the location of the Wellington crash in Milford Docks. The buildings have long gone as part of the complete redevelopment of the area. *Author's Collection*

The *West Wales Guardian* report, written under strict wartime censorship, was brief and gave little information away:

'Six men were killed in an accident at Milford Haven last week. Considerable damage was done by the accident and good service was put in by a number of local people and members of the Services. Unfortunately, their efforts did not result in the rescue of any of the men involved. None of the men were from the locality'.

For those living outside of the Milford Haven area more questions were asked than answered by the report. But Milford residents were all to grimly aware of the untold story behind the news paragraph. They

had seen or heard of the aftermath of the accident, realised its human toll and marvelled at the town's lucky escape from an even greater disaster.

The six men were crew of a twin-engined Wellington bomber which crashed near Milford's fish dock in the early hours of Sunday July 19th 1942. One of the most widely produced of RAF types, the

Sergeant Keith James Bradley.
Daphne Glen

Sergeant Edward Douglas Reginald Jennings.
Lillian Jamieson

Sergeant George Ernest Warburton.
Lillian Jamieson

Cap flashes... Three of the young Australian airmen who lost their lives in the Wellington. All wear white flashes in their forage caps, identifying them as aircrew under training.

Wellington was extensively used for training and the crew was on a flight from their base at RAF Lichfield in Staffordshire, the home of No 27 Operational Training Unit.

An all-NCO crew, they had been briefed for a six-hour night cross-country exercise with take-off at 2315 hours on the Saturday. Their route was Base - Rhyl - Calf of Man - St Davids Head - Mull of Galloway - St Bees Head - Rhyl - Base. Sadly, they only got as far as Pembrokeshire.

Ministry of Defence records state that 'it appeared that the Wellington was in distress because it was reported at 0234 hours that the IFF of the aircraft was on SOS. The searchlight pointer organisation attempted to home the aircraft to Talbenny, but it overshot the aerodrome and crashed near the docks'. (IFF was the Identification Friend or Foe equipment aboard).

Milford Haven Docks Police Sergeant Stanley Roberts was on duty that night and vividly recalled the accident. On his retirement in 1979 he told Ethel Clark, the well-remembered Milford Haven reporter for the *West Wales Guardian*: 'I heard an aircraft making a helluva noise and thought at first it was one of the old Walrus seaplanes from Pembroke Dock. Then I realised it was flying on one engine. I knocked on the office window of the Docks Manager, Mr J. C. Ward, who was on fire-watching duties, and told him there was something wrong. With that the crippled Wellington is believed to have touched the old Ice Factory stack before crashing on the docks on the paint and oil stores of Mr E. E. Carter's Westward Trawlers.

'The aircraft buried its nose in the earthbank below the Marine Gardens houses, exploded and burst into flames. There were only two of us at the scene at first - we did what we could to stop the fire spreading. It was an awful tragedy but the lucky thing was that the bomber did not crash on top of the local homes.'

There were other reports that the aircraft was firing red Very pistol flares as an obvious sign of distress and stories circulated that the pilot, desperately looking for somewhere to land, may have mistaken the recently re-roofed Fishmarket for a runway. What really happened in those last minutes will never be known.

In the light of dawn the grim reality became all too apparent, and revealed just how close Milford Haven had been from an even bigger disaster. A few feet higher and the aircraft would have impacted in Hamilton Terrace which overlooks the waterway.

The crew of Wellington N2749 consisted of five Australians and one Englishman. The captain was Sergeant Kenneth Steinbach, the only married member and the oldest at 29.

Another of the Australians was 23-year-old Sergeant George Warburton. He was not a member of the Steinbach crew but volunteered to fly with them that night in order to get a few more navigational 'star shots'. George had trained in Canada with his good friend Sergeant Douglas Jennings who died alongside him.

RAF Pembroke Dock took charge of the Wellington crew and it was from the flying-boat station that the funerals were held. All five Australians were buried with full military honours at the Military Cemetery at Llanion, Pembroke Dock.

Sergeant Warren Jarrett, another friend of George Warburton and Douglas Jennings, wrote to the Warburton family in the August: 'I was told indirectly that the boys were given a very large and sympathetic funeral. None of us who knew them was able to go.'

The sixth member of the crew, 20-year-old Sergeant Maurice Cooke, was taken to his home area for burial at New Bradwell, Buckinghamshire.

The Wellington came down very close to Marine Gardens and the residents of this street, greatly touched by the tragedy on their doorstep, organised a collection which soon totalled £28. This was forwarded to the RAF's Bomber Command with the

In Canada... Wearing their new sergeants' stripes and Observers' half wings, Douglas Jennings (left) and George Warburton (centre) are joined by Warren Jarrett. This picture was taken in early 1942 as they completed their training in Canada. *Lillian Jamieson*

Services... The coffins of the five Australians are carried from the impressive RAF Church at Pembroke Dock's flying-boat station following a service there. A second service took place at St Mary's Roman Catholic Church in the town before burial at the Military Cemetery at Llanion. *Lillian Jamieson*

request that it be sent to the dependants of those who lost their lives at Milford Haven.

Mrs S. Phillips, 6 Marine Gardens - whose husband and three sons were in uniform serving in the Royal Navy and the trawler fleet - had the initial idea for a collection. She was helped by Mrs J. Phillips and Miss Olga Jenkins, Marine Gardens, and Miss Audrey Winstanley, Precelly Place.

In the months that followed letters were exchanged between Milford Haven and the airmen's families in Australia. And in response to a request for information on the accident Mrs Phillips wrote a revealing letter to the parents and the families of the Australians.

Recalling that the crash occurred at 2.50 am (official records say 3.08 am), Mrs Phillips went on: 'I happened to be downstairs at the time when suddenly I heard a plane making a terrible noise coming towards my house. It just skimmed my roof, dislodging a few slates and then I heard a terrible crash.

'There were soldiers, first aid men, firemen and hundreds of others but nobody could do anything except the firemen with their hoses. I feel sure they crashed where they did to avoid coming on our houses. If they had gone on another couple of seconds they would have come down in the river and I am sure, if they had, some of them would have been saved.'

The crash of Wellington N2749 - and Milford's amazing escape - were well known to members of the newly formed Pembrokeshire Aviation Group and so it was a logical step for the Group to consider marking this wartime accident with a memorial. In early 1986 the decision was taken to arrange a commemoration to coincide with the 44th anniversary of the crash.

Despite the short timescale considerable progress was made in contacting relatives and friends of the aircrew. Four of the families in Australia were contacted using a variety of means, including newspaper appeals, and all were most supportive of the Group's memorial plans. Only the family of pilot Ken Steinbach could not be traced - despite great efforts in Queensland where his wartime address had been.

Thanks also to Bletchley RAFA Branch contact was made with the family of Maurice Cooke and arrangements were made for a service to take place at New Bradwell Cemetery to coincide with the commemorations at Milford Haven.

And publicity in Pembrokeshire also identified the exact location of the crash. This was pinpointed by former teacher Mr Tom Martin, of Broad Haven, who in 1942 had been a clerk employed by trawler owners in the fishing port.

On Friday July 18th 1986 - just one day before the 50th anniversary - a large crowd gathered on Hamilton Terrace for the open air service, conducted by the Vicar of Milford Haven, Canon Geoffrey Thomas. The bronze plaque, recording the aircraft, date of the accident and names of the crew, was unveiled by Mr Bill Shenfield, Chairman of the Milford Haven Branch, Royal British Legion, which had generously paid for the plaque. It was mounted on a slate-topped plinth built by Preseli District Council close to the imposing war memorial.

As a spectacular finale to this service the present-day Royal Air Force paid their own tribute with flypasts of formations of four Jet Provosts and four Hawks from RAF Brawdy.

This was part one of the commemoration. The party moved on to Pembroke Dock's Military Cemetery where an equally moving service took place. The Rev Alan Thomas, Vicar of Pembroke Dock, officiated and a wreath from the Pembroke and Pembroke Dock Branch, Royal British Legion, was laid by Brigadier Cliff Gough while the RAFA Dedication was spoken by Ken Phillips, President of 648 Branch of RAFA.

Here, too, a very personal tribute was made on behalf of the fiancee of Sergeant George Warburton, the young Observer who had gone on the final flight to take more 'star sights'.

Unveiling... The memorial plaque on Hamilton Terrace was unveiled by Mr Bill Shenfield, President of the Milford Haven Branch, Royal British Legion, in July 1986. Pictured by the memorial are, left to right: Canon Geoffrey Thomas, Vicar of Milford Haven; Mr Bill Shenfield; Councillor and Mrs David Adams, Milford Haven's Mayor and Mayoress; Councillor Gordon Cawood, Chairman, Preseli District Council; John Evans and John Banner, Pembrokeshire Aviation Group. *Western Telegraph*

Legion... Brigadier Cliff Gough, of the Pembroke and Pembroke Dock Branch, Royal British Legion, lays a wreath during the impressive service at the Military Cemetery, Pembroke Dock. *Western Telegraph*

From faraway New South Wales Miss Lillian Jamieson sent a personal message and verses from the Bible which she requested be placed, together with a single red rose, on George Warburton's grave. This was carried out by the Aviation Group's John Banner.

Since 1986 the Pembrokeshire Aviation Group has continued to remember the Wellington crew and has particularly marked the 50th and 60th anniversaries of the crash. In July 1992 a wreath was laid at the Hamilton Terrace memorial on behalf of the Group by former Wellington navigator Len Warlow and representatives of the local Royal British Legion Branch attended alongside PAG members.

In July 2002 the Group was joined by three members of the RAF Lichfield Association - Norman Corbett, George Myatt and Chris Pointon - and representatives of the Legion Branch for a short service at the memorial. Floral tributes were also laid on the graves in Pembroke Dock.

Over the years, too, relatives and friends of the

Australian airmen have made special visits to Pembrokeshire and have linked up with Aviation Group members. The Group is appreciative of the great support given by all the families.

Crew list: Sergeant Kenneth Henry Charles Steinbach, RAAF, pilot, aged 29, son of Henry Walter and Mercy Steinbach; husband of Daphne Alberta Steinbach, of Ipswich, Queensland

Sergeant Keith James Bradley, RAAF, Wireless Operator/Air Gunner, aged 25, son of James Albert and Alice Maud Bradley, of Five Dock, New South Wales

Sergeant William Harry Condon, RAAF, Observer, aged 22, son of James Benedict and Lillian Norris Condon, of Laverton, Victoria

Sergeant Maurice Cooke, RAF, Air Gunner, aged 20, son of Frederick John and Marguerite Cooke of New Bradwell, Buckinghamshire

Sergeant Edward Douglas Reginald Jennings, RAAF, Air Observer, aged 26, son of Reginald Webb and Madeline Lucy Jennings, of Strathfield, New South Wales

Sergeant George Ernest Warburton, RAAF, Observer, aged 23, son of Ernest Alfred and Elizabeth Iolet Warburton, of Turramurra, New South Wales.

Lichfield trio...
The Wellington crew had flown from RAF Lichfield, Staffordshire. Sixty years on - in July 2002 - three members of the RAF Lichfield Association joined Pembrokeshire Aviation Group members to honour the crew. The Lichfield trio are seen by some of the War Graves at the Military Cemetery - Norman Corbett (left), Chris Pointon and George Myatt (right). *Author*

CHAPTER VII

A few feet too low
Consolidated Liberator GR VI EV881, September 19th 1944

Codes... A fine study of a 547 Squadron Liberator in flight, carrying the squadron code letters 2V. This is actually KG869, a sister aircraft to EV881. No photograph of EV881 has been traced although the Imperial War Museum's archive includes a fine shot of EV882. *Danny Quinn*

The sounds of aerial activity were a constant part of life in wartime Britain. Often, as the war wore on, people on the ground hardly gave a second glance as yet another aircraft appeared in the skies overhead.

Even in remote and rural parts of Pembrokeshire the steady drone of aircraft was an everyday sound.

But on one September night in 1944 the sound of one heavy aircraft passing overhead was followed abruptly by that of a crash.

Families in the scattered farms below the southern slopes of the Preseli Hills peered out from behind the blackout to see a fire on the ridge above.

Leigh Light...
The underwing housing of the Leigh Light is shown prominently in this shot of a 206 Squadron aircraft.
Danny Quinn

Those nearest to the crash site hastened to make the steep climb up on to Carn Bica, one of the highest of the Preseli tops.

In those split seconds a four-engined Liberator had struck the ground just below the ridge. A few feet higher and the big bomber would have escaped unscathed. It was not to be.

Also in those seconds five members of the crew had died, and the other four were injured. And within hours one of the survivors would succumb to his injuries.

Telephone calls were made to the police and the RAF at Withybush, Haverfordwest - the nearest RAF station - was informed. An all too familiar pattern which followed aircraft accidents was put into action.

The aircraft was a Liberator GR VI of No 547 Squadron, based at St Eval in Cornwall. The GR stood for General Reconnaissance and reflected the squadron's maritime role within 19 Group of Coastal Command.

The Liberators were sprouting underwing searchlights as 547 Squadron was in the process of converting from a day maritime role to night attack. The searchlights - known as Leigh Lights after their inventor - were a powerful weapon in the war against the German U-boat. In conjunction with radar carried on the aircraft the Leigh Lights were able to turn night into day on any submarines they came upon.

For 547 Squadron the use of this new equipment meant that constant practice was required to hone the skills of operating the radar and Leigh Lights and attack procedures.

At St Eval on the afternoon of September 19th Stan Kearey and his crew were off duty. They had only completed a nine hour anti-submarine patrol the previous day, returning to base at 3.15 am, and were not on stand-by for flying. All that changed when the Royal Navy offered the use of one of its submarines for an exercise. This was an opportunity to get in some quality practice against almost the 'real thing'.

Warrant Officer Kearey and his crew were called up at short notice and began the sequence of preparation for a flight - collecting personal

Snapshot...
Stan Kearey in a snapshot taken when training at North Battleford, Saskatchewan, Canada, in March 1942. This was before he got his sergeant's stripes and coveted pilot's wings. At the Court of Inquiry following the crash it was stated that Stan Kearey had flown a total of 1,232 hours of which 253 were on Liberators.
Margaret Rumens

Having hurriedly moved to the new aircraft they completed their pre-flight checks and finally lifted off the St Eval runway. A Navy submarine was waiting.

In the meantime Danny Quinn had returned from town to find, unusually, that his hut was empty. On his way to the Sergeants' Mess he was told that his crew had been called out - 'I was astonished as it was so soon after completing an ops flight.'

Danny tried his best to catch up with his crew but to no avail. He was bitterly disappointed to have missed the trip and felt guilty too. He returned to

equipment, rations and parachutes, and attending briefings on the exercise and weather. All members of the crew were contacted except for one - air gunner Danny Quinn was in town at the laundry.

The other nine members of Kearey's crew went to their allocated aircraft. Then they hit a snag. The Liberator was unserviceable so they had to switch to another aircraft - EV881. They had previously flown in EV881 on a training flight on the 16th.

Training... Smiles all round as Stan Kearey is joined by seven other members of his crew after they came together at No 111 OTU in the Bahamas, following earlier training in Canada. Back row, left to right: Alec Campbell, Stan Kearey, one of the original navigators (believed to be A. Begg), Ray Sellors, John Boyd. Front row, left to right: Robert Evans, Ted Moody, Billy Soroski. *George Jared*

Robert Evans, Wireless Operator Mechanic.
Norman Evans

Albert Humphreys, Air Gunner.
George Jared

Ray Sellors, Flight Engineer.
The Sellors Family

Richard Shearly, Navigator.
Richard Shearly

the mess, played a game of darts or billiards and had an early night.

Forty years on he was to recall: 'Waking rather early the following morning I found the crew had not returned and wondered what had gone wrong. Looking on the bright side I thought it possible they had landed at another base. Then I remember a friend, Gordon Berryman, leaning through the hut window and, after a pause, telling me the news - Stan Kearey's crew had crashed late yesterday in the Welsh hills. What a shock.'

Two days later a very sad Danny flew in an Anson with the Squadron Adjutant, Squadron Leader Dick, to RAF Haverfordwest and both were taken to the nearby RAF hospital to visit the survivors.

Again two days later - on September 23rd - Danny and the Adjutant flew to Haverfordwest via St Athan, near Cardiff, to attend the funeral service for the four crewmen who were buried with full military honours at City Road Cemetery, Haverfordwest. Here they met Stan Kearey's

In the team... Individual studies of four of the close knit team who flew in Liberator EV881 on its final flight.

parents and other relatives - it was a sad day for the young air gunner and all involved.

City Road Cemetery is the last resting place for two Canadians, Warrant Officer Billy Soroski and Flight Sergeant John Duncan Boyd, and two RAF crewmen, Flight Sergeant Robert Evans and Sergeant Albert Humphries. At just 19 Albert was the youngest in the crew.

Stan Kearey is buried at his home town of Farnham, Surrey, while Flight Engineer Ray Sellors, who hailed from Yorkshire, was taken for burial at Bentley-with-Arksey New Cemetery, near Doncaster. Apart from his parents and sister Stan Kearey was mourned by his new bride - he had married just three weeks earlier.

The crash of EV881 merited a short entry in the Squadron's Operational Record Book for September. 'At approximately 2250 hours on September 19th, during the hours of darkness, aircraft EV881, captained by W/O Kearey, flew into the crest of a hill 4 miles N E of Maenclochog, S. Wales. The a/c caught fire and W/O Kearey and four of the crew were killed; another died in hospital and the remaining three were injured and detained in hospital. The cause of the accident is believed to be an error of navigation as the crew was briefed to proceed to an 'Oasthouse' exercise via the Smalls Light'.

The ORB also recorded that Leigh Light training had continued and was completed by the end of the month when the Squadron was considered fully operational on Leigh Lights. But this had come at a price.

In an ORB record of EV881's crew Robert Evans is listed as died in hospital on September 20th as a result of injuries sustained in the accident but his Commonwealth War Graves headstone at Haverfordwest gives the date as September 19th. Locally, too, burial records list the 19th. This anomaly is something that has yet to be drawn to the relevant authorities.

As was the case in such accidents a court of inquiry was held. According to Wreckovery writer David Smith the court of inquiry found that the altimeter had been set wrongly and was reading too high.

For the Author the first knowledge of EV881's crash came from a booklet entitled *High Ground Wrecks*, published in the 1970s by the same David Smith. It listed three wreck sites in the Preseli Hills. During a visit to the site with Air Training Corps cadets in the early 1980s sizeable pieces of wreckage and bits of equipment were found in an area where, so many years on after the crash, still no vegetation was growing. This visit was the first of many to EV881's crash site and the start of a long and fascinating research road.

In early 1984, with the 40th anniversary of the

Died for His Country

W.O.I B. W. SOROSKI

21, who was killed September 19 during air operations over enemy territory, according to official word received by his brother, A. Soroski, Barry Hotel. Funeral services were held Saturday, September 23, and burial was in Wales. Born in Saskatoon, "Billy" Soroski attended Princess Alexandra School and Technical Collegiate. He enlisted in the R.C.A.F. at Saskatoon in September, 1941. He took his wireless training at Calgary and graduated as an air gunner at Macdonald. After service in the West Indies, he proceeded overseas in May this year. In addition to his brother, he is survived by his mother, Mrs. M. Soroski, North Battleford, and a sister, Mrs. A. Fitchett, Winnipeg.

Liberator crash looming, four work colleagues and aviation enthusiasts in Haverfordwest began casually discussing the idea of putting a memorial on the site. Soon this became a definite goal and tasks were allocated within a tight timescale. Out of this the Pembrokeshire Aviation Group was born.

Malcolm Cullen, Ieuan Griffiths and the Author - then all working for the Pembrokeshire Coast National Park Department - and Derek Rees, working in the same building for Dyfed County Council's Highways Department, set to with a will and soon a picture began emerging of the last fateful flight of EV881 and of its crew.

Appeals in newspapers all over the country reaped rewards, a key contact being former 547 Squadron aircrewman Gordon Berryman who was in touch with Danny Quinn. A letter to Danny's home in France - where he worked for the Commonwealth War Graves Commission - brought an instant response, and a collection of photos.

In the summer weeks much of the spare time of the four Group members was devoted to the EV881 project. Contact with the recently formed 547 Squadron Association proved fruitful and pages from the Squadron ORBs were obtained.

There were four Canadians among the crew. The Author's cousin Brian James, living in Saskatoon, Canada, spent hours phoning every Soroski in the local telephone book, sadly without linking in to the family of Billy Soroski. But he did find a newspaper cutting reporting on the death of the local airmen far away 'during air operations over enemy territory'.

Other Canadian appeals were, in time, to bring about contact with survivors Ted Moody and Richard Shearly - the latter living in California. No contact could be established with the family of John Duncan Boyd.

A newspaper appeal in Surrey brought contact with Stan Kearey's mother and sister; an item in a Liverpool paper led to the Evans family getting in touch and finally a link up was made with the family of Albert Humphries. Initially the search had concentrated in the Ammanford area named as Albert's home area. It later transpired that Albert had been evacuated with his mother to Llandybie earlier in the war before joining the RAF when he was old enough. Finally the family was traced to Sussex. Pieces of a large jigsaw were coming together quickly.

The involvement of No 592 Branch of RAFA at Haverfordwest - where PAG member Derek Rees was also Branch Chairman - proved vitally important. Derek took on the heavy responsibility of co-ordinating the arrangements for the services on the 40th anniversary. And the presence in Pembrokeshire of a major RAF station - Brawdy - was another key factor.

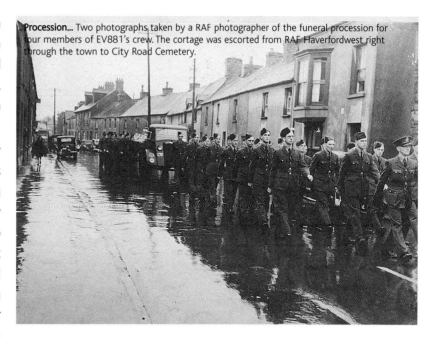

Procession... Two photographs taken by a RAF photographer of the funeral procession for four members of EV881's crew. The cortage was escorted from RAF Haverfordwest right through the town to City Road Cemetery.

Top: In heavy rain the escort party of airmen marched through the main street of Prendergast, Haverfordwest, on September 24th 1944. *George Jared*

Above: The four coffins were carried into City Road Cemetery where the service was conducted by RAF padre Squadron Leader Cole. *George Jared*

Standards... The Standards of ex-Service organisations flew proudly as the two clergy led the service at City Road Cemetery exactly 40 years on. *Western Telegraph*

All the planning, discussions and arrangements were put to the test on Wednesday September 19th 1984 at services and ceremonies in Haverfordwest and in the Preseli Hills.

At City Road Cemetery the Padres of RAF Brawdy, the Rev Richard Rees of Solva and Father Michael Myerscough, St Davids, conducted a moving service of remembrance which was attended by civic leaders, service personnel, representatives of many organisations and cadet forces.

Honoured guests were Mrs Margaret Rumens, sister of Stan Kearey, and George Jared, brother of Albert Humphries, who were joined by Danny Quinn and two other members of the 547 Squadron Association, Len Brockwell and Bob Denwood.

Flowers were laid on the graves of the four Liberator crewmen while Legion poppy crosses were placed on all the service graves. Among those carrying out this duty were Haverfordwest's Mayor and other civic heads; the CO of RAF Brawdy, Group Captain Mike Gibson; the President and Chairman of 592 Branch RAFA, Bill Nicholas and Derek Rees, and representatives of other service organisations and ATC squadrons.

The serving RAF paid their own unique tribute as four Hawk jets from Brawdy swept low overhead under grey skies, the formation led by Wing Commander Brian Hoskins, a former leader of the Red Arrows display team.

And as the standards from RAFA and Royal British Legion branches dipped in salute the Last Post and Reveille were played by four trumpeters from the Mary Immaculate Band, a fitting finale to an impressive service.

All this was a prelude to a visit to the crash site, a RAF bus taking many of the guests up into the hills. Below Carn Bica members of the Maenclochog Royal British Legion branch had assembled, along with local people, some of whom had first-hand memories of that wartime night. Dozens of people made the stiff climb up to the site where a second service was conducted by the RAF padres assisted by the Rev Anthony Bailey, Priest-in-charge of Mynachlogddu.

A temporary plaque bearing the names of the Liberator crew was placed on the site and Margaret Rumens laid a wreath of red roses. This was an exact copy of one made in 1944 and placed then on the graves at City Road Cemetery. It was made by Mrs Hilda Turley of Haverfordwest who 40 years earlier had made the original.

It was an especially poignant pilgrimage for the relatives of the two crewmen and for Danny Quinn who had long vowed to visit the site of the crash. And it also brought back vivid memories for the Chairman of Preseli District Council, Councillor

Dedication... The four founder members of the Pembrokeshire Aviation Group are pictured with the Rev Anthony Bailey after the permanent memorial was dedicated in 1985. Left to right: John Evans, Derek Rees, Malcolm Cullen, the Rev Anthony Bailey and Ieuan Griffiths. *Author's Collection*

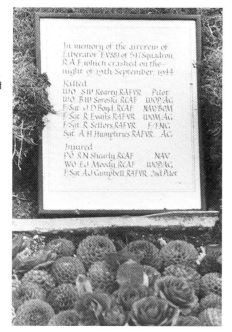

Floral... The temporary memorial left on the Carn Bica site, framed by a piece of metal from the Liberator. In front is the lovely floral tribute which replicated that made in 1944 for the funeral service in Haverfordwest. *Author's Collection*

Desmond Codd. In 1944 he had been farming in the valley below and came up to the site the following day.

The 40th anniversary events were just the beginning of a remarkable story which, more than 20 years on, still endures. In that time the Pembrokeshire Aviation Group has grown substantially in numbers, carried out several other commemorations and projects, and has kept returning on a regular basis to Carn Bica.

In 1985 the permanent memorial was dedicated on site by the Rev Anthony Bailey, Priest-in-charge of Mynachlogddu. The brass plaque was made at RAF St Athan for RAF Brawdy and was set in a simple stone cairn which was built by the indefatigable Derek Rees. One of RAF Brawdy's Sea King search and rescue helicopters provided the lift to the area for

Reunion... EV881's three survivors and crewmate Danny Quinn were re-united for the first time at the 547 Squadron Association Reunion in London in 1987. Left to right: Alec Campbell, Ted Moody, Richard Shearly and Danny Quinn. *Danny Quinn*

heavier items like sand and cement.

Strong links were maintained with the 547 Squadron Association, the original PAG 'gang of four' becoming honorary members of the association and attending squadron reunions. In September 1986 several members of 547 Association visited Pembrokeshire and a simple service was held at the Carn Bica cairn.

Research, too, continued in the UK and overseas resulting in contacts with the family of Ray Sellors and with the three survivors, residing respectively in Canada, the USA and Australia. Thanks to the Group's efforts all three survivors - Alec Campbell, Ted Moody and Richard Shearly - and Danny Quinn

were able to meet up at a 547 Squadron Reunion in London in 1987. In advance of the reunion Ted Moody and members of his family made a very brief visit to west Wales but time did not allow for a trip to the memorial.

Over the years many visits to the memorial have been made in the company of relatives and friends of various members of the Liberator crew and special commemorative events have marked the 50th and 60th anniversaries. The heightened interest in the story behind the Carn Bica memorial has brought many more people to the Preselis in search of the site and gradually the large number of metal parts which existed have diminished. Pieces of fused metal though still remain around the brass plaque testifying to the ferocity of the fire which followed the impact.

In June 1999 the Author had a surprise visitor - Richard Shearly, one of the survivors. Richard had flown from California to attend a 547 Squadron Reunion and had travelled on to Pembrokeshire especially to visit the site of his crash. The following day he braved unseasonal weather to walk up to the memorial - nearly 55 years had elapsed since that wartime night when EV881 came to grief on a Preseli ridge.

Of all the stories associated with the Liberator and its crew none is more remarkable than that concerning a signet ring. It all began when a family out walking on the hills came by the memorial. In a radio interview Flight Sergeant Dave Pengilly, then RAF Brawdy's Community Relations Officer, recalled how it had all developed.

The Knight family children had been looking around the site and one of them spotted something bright on the ground. When dad was called over he ran his hand through the area and found a signet ring, almost perfect apart from a small crack. And the ring was marked with the initials S W K.

The ring found its way to RAF Brawdy and Dave Pengilly contacted the PAG's Malcolm Cullen who could immediately say that S W K referred to Stan Kearey. Contact with sister Margaret Rumens confirmed the link as Margaret and Stan had each been presented with a ring by their parents at the same time.

Margaret wore hers every day and on her next visit to Pembrokeshire in September 1990, to coincide with the 46th anniversary of EV881's crash, she was presented with Stan's signet ring at the EV881 memorial by Group Captain Tim Webb, CO of RAF Brawdy. She immediately placed it on the finger next to her own.

Crew list: Killed: Warrant Officer Stanley William Kearey, RAFVR, Pilot, aged 23, son of Mr and Mrs Kearey, of Farnham, Surrey

Flight Sergeant John Duncan Boyd, RCAF, Navigator/Bomber, aged 27, son of Samuel and Annie Maude Boyd of Mimico, Ontario, Canada

Flight Sergeant Robert Evans, RAFVR, Wireless Operator Mechanic/Air Gunner, aged 21, son of Joseph Henry Evans and Margaret Evans of Bootle, near Liverpool

Sergeant Albert Henry Humphries, RAFVR, Air Gunner, aged 19, son of Mrs A. Jared of Llandybie, Carmarthenshire

Flight Sergeant Raymond Sellors, RAF, Flight Engineer, aged 21, son of Frederick and Jane Annie Sellors, of Bentley, Doncaster

Warrant Officer Billy William Soroski, RCAF, Wireless Operator/Air Gunner, aged 22, son of Fred and Mary Soroski, of Saskatoon, Saskatchewan, Canada

Injured: Flight Sergeant Alec Campbell, RAFVR, 2nd Pilot

Pilot Officer Richard Shearly, RCAF, Navigator

Warrant Officer Edward Moody, RCAF, Wireless Operator/Air Gunner

*Grid reference of the EV881 site is SN 127318.

Half century... A special visit was made to the Liberator memorial in September 1994, marking the 50th anniversary of the crash. Here relatives of three of the crew join together at the memorial. Left to right: Richard Evans, Lily Allin (sister of Ray Sellors), Lyn Evans, Norman Evans (brother of Robert Evans), George Jared (brother of Albert Humphreys, and Anne Jared. *Author*

Survivors' stories

In the late 1980s first-hand accounts were penned by all three survivors in response to letters written by a teenage aviation enthusiast. Jonathan Teasdale, from London, regularly spent holidays in Pembrokeshire with his family and after visiting the memorial on one of the trips, and making contact with the Aviation Group, he wrote to the survivors.

Ted Moody

Our crew was probably a typical bunch of guys from such places as Saskatchewan, Quebec, Surrey and Yorkshire - many different backgrounds and accents but having been thrown together in the RAF we had an incredibly close relationship that I suspect is peculiar to any wartime situation.

We had chosen our crew in Nassau, The Bahamas, and were determined to prove that a bunch of NCOs could hack it with commissioned ranks any day of the week. We were all in the same billets, mess and were virtually inseparable from then on.

Our operational training lasted three months. Our first kite was the B-25 Mitchell, mainly chosen for its excellent flying and high performance capabilities and to get us used to the feel of what was to come - the Liberator.

After our OTU we went back to Dorval, Montreal, and were ordered to pick up a Lib in Bermuda that had developed leaky tanks on the way over from the States. It was repaired, we flew to the Azores and then to Prestwick, then Bournemouth, then to St Eval for ops.

St Eval was a really busy place in early spring of 1944. We had four squadrons of B-24s doing radar coverage of the Bay of Biscay and the English Channel between the Scilly Isles and Ushant, off the French coast.

We started our ops and after the usual dumb things developed into a reasonably good crew, full of beans and quietly confident that we could take on anyone our size or larger.

Our NCO status was rudely interrupted by the news that our crew was now to include a second navigator and this was where Dick Shearly came into the picture. However, with good humour we accepted this gangly P/O and he turned out to be a terrific guy. D-Day came and went and the work and patrols went on. We seemed to get better.

Then came the 'Oasthouse' affair. 'Oasthouse' was a series of exercises devised by the Admiralty and the RAF to again sharpen our skills and techniques and included a new type of camera that seemed to have some advanced technology for recording results of submarine attack.

On the 19th we were briefed, allotted one kite, moved to another and took off to practice with the RN sub. The weather at take off wasn't too bad, some cloud, very dark but flyable.

Our track took us from St Eval north over Wales and up to the Irish Sea. Everything was okay, the plane seemed to be in good shape and we settled in to what seemed to be a milk run.

I was listening out on the radio to group frequency with my back to the front of the aircraft. The radio operator's position had a large seat with a high metal back and well padded - possibly the combination of these two factors helped to save my life.

All of a sudden there was an incredible explosion when we hit the mountain. Luckily I was still conscious and had the presence of mind to inflate my Mae West lifejacket. This gave me added body protection as I was still inside the kite being bounced all over the place.

I must have been knocked out momentarily because when I came to some of my clothing was beginning to burn and my hands and hair were starting to sizzle.

Thinking about discretion and valour and all that stuff, I decided to get out of the wreck which was burning furiously (we were carrying about 1,500 gallons of gas). I ran a few steps and passed out on a hill near the burning plane. It was pitch black; I didn't

Remembered... Relatives of two of EV881's crew - pilot Stan Kearey and flight engineer Ray Sellors - were joined by Pembrokeshire Aviation Group members and friends on the 60th anniversary of the accident, September 2004. *Author*

see or hear any of the other guys so thought that they had all been killed. In my semi-conscious state I thought I heard some crying but learned later that it was sheep maimed by the crash.

Some local people came up the mountain and found me and did all they could to help me and some of the other survivors.

We were taken by ambulance to the local hospital where our wounds were treated and then flown to St Athan RAF hospital.

I was depressed for some time about losing our really good crew. However, life goes on and after a hospital stay was sent on leave and then posted to Leuchars (in Scotland) where the squadron had been transferred.

I finished up my tour with another crew and came home (to Canada) and flew with a reserve squadron in Alberta for some time.

Richard Shearly

We did not normally fly the same aircraft on each mission but took the one assigned to us. No 547 Squadron was in the process of converting from a daylight to a night anti-U-boat squadron and that was the reason for our exercise. It is true that we had short notice but this did not seem strange to any of us at the time.

During the exercise Johnnie Boyd and I would have taken turns operating Leigh Light controls to spot a British submarine in the Irish Sea. This was an exercise which allowed the radar operator and the Leigh Light operator to practice finding a U-boat on the surface, charging its batteries, at night. This was to be our first exercise with a submarine although we had had previous exercises finding buoys. It was not easy.

I was sitting in the nose of the Lib with Johnnie, our other navigator, waiting to arrive at the submarine sanctuary to begin practicing. We had two navigators because normally our patrols were long and we would each navigate half a patrol. I had no warning of the impending crash. In fact, I had no indication that the crash had occurred. At the time I never knew what

happened; I went out like a light. Why Johnnie died and I survived I'll never know.

After the crash I was unconscious for a couple of days and by the time I regained consciousness the other two survivors had been moved to other hospitals. I was visited by an Air Force investigator who asked me many questions regarding the circumstances leading up to the crash. I understand a report was prepared.

Alex Campbell and Ted Moody recovered and returned to 547 Squadron. By the time I got out of the hospitals the war in Europe was over. Alec's parents were very kind to me. They travelled all the way from south of London to my second hospital in south east Wales to visit me. Later, when I was mobile, they had me to their home a couple of times.

I don't know what caused the crash but one must consider that we were not used to flying at night over blacked-out (wartime) land. It has been by far the most traumatic experience of my life. Apart from the physical and mental trauma of the crash itself, there was the loss of six very close friends.

Alec Campbell

We had been on operations the previous night flying a patrol blocking the entrance to the English Channel between Lands End and Brest, the object being to deny access to the waters off Normandy to German U-boats.

The U-boats used to surface during darkness to recharge their batteries. We could pick them up using our radar, home in on them dropping down during the attack run from 1,000 ft (our usual patrol height) to 50 ft to drop a stick of depth charges. The Leigh Light was used to identify the target and for, in theory, any minor corrections to the bombing run. Of course, as soon as the light came on the U-boat would start firing back so in practice the light was only put on in the last half mile of the run, everything up to that time being done on radar.

The Leigh Light was a standard naval searchlight (built of brass and bronze) mounted in a faired nacelle outboard of No 4 engine. There was a type of joystick to control it up and down and left and right. It had to be trained on the target before illumination. The aircraft had to be steady on the radar altimeter at between 50 and 100 ft and the drift angle was established from the chart of the radar operator.

All this of course required immaculate instrument flying and great team work and the type of attack was practiced constantly at night and that was what the Oasthouse exercise was all about. We were to rendezvous with a RN submarine and carry out dummy attacks.

Normally practice was against a towed target and a practice period with a real sub had never occurred before. There was a reason for this - the Germans had developed the 'schnorkel' to allow the subs to remain at periscope depth and draw air for the diesel engines through the schnorkel tube. I gather the submarine we were to rendezvous with had been fitted with a mock-up schnorkel and part of the exercise was to see how easy or difficult it was to pick up with our 3 cm radar.

As a crew we were briefed for the exercise but the original aircraft became unserviceable and we had to change to EV881. This of course caused a delay and to make up time it was decided to fly direct to the rendezvous instead of up the Irish Sea and round to the north of Rathlin Island. This is what led to the crash; we didn't intend to fly over the Preseli Hills but to be a few miles to the west.

It was a very dark night and I saw nothing before the crash but woke up on the hillside having been thrown clear with the aircraft

Swift to Strike... The crest of No 547 Squadron depicting a kingfisher diving. The Latin motto means 'Swift to Strike'. *Author's Collection*

in flames alongside of me. In a very short time some helpers arrived (I don't know how long I was knocked out) but as I came to somebody was asking me if there were any bombs aboard. There were only 14 lb practice bombs on for the exercise but they and thousands of rounds of ammunition going off added hell to the scene of a fiercely burning Liberator.

I was helped walk down the hill to I don't know where but it was a small cottage hospital. Four of us survived but Bob Evans died of his injuries.

From there to hospital at RAF Haverfordwest and then to the burns unit. A few months later it was back to the squadron, now at Leuchars. I formed my own crew and it was back to long range patrols in the Denmark Straits and between Northern Scotland and Iceland, and later in the Skagerak and Kattegat. Then it was all over.

CHAPTER VIII

Farmyard fatalities
Consolidated Liberator Mk VIII KH183, July 8th 1945

Workhorse... An example of a Liberator Mk VIII, similar to the one whch crashed by Emlych Farm. A workhorse in all theatres of operation, the GR Mk VIII was the last version of nearly 1,700 of the type delivered to the RAF. *Royal Air Force Museum P6561*

LIBERATOR G. R. MK.
TWIN WASP
AUGUST 1944

The war in Europe may finally have ended in May 1945 but in the Far East there was still much work to do. The Allies' focus could now be concentrated upon the war against Japan. With the atomic bomb a very closely guarded secret it looked like being a long, hard and costly slog.

Many of the aircrew and groundcrew involved in the war against Germany now found themselves marked up for new roles to be played out in the Far East. Like many other units the Sunderland flying-boat squadrons at Pembroke Dock were quickly run down, both Nos 228 RAF and 461 RAAF disbanding in the weeks following VE-Day, their Coastal Command duties done.

For airmen not tour expired or due for early release, postings came through to other units. Many former Sunderland aircrew were destined to fly Liberator transports and were posted to former Coastal Command squadrons operating the big four-engined bombers.

At RAF St Davids in June 1945 No 53 Squadron, recently operating maritime patrol Liberators out of Iceland, moved in to take up a new role in Transport Command. Training began immediately including night flying.

The aircraft were Mark VIIIs which were stripped of guns and fitted out for their new transport duties. One of these was KH183 which on the night of July 7th/8th was allocated to a four-man crew including three who had recently transferred from No 228 Squadron. They were detailed to carry out night circuits and landings on the airfield.

What began as normal training routine quickly turned to disaster. At 3.25 am, just two minutes after lifting off from the runway, the Liberator crashed near the airfield, caught fire and was burnt out.

Sunderlanders... Charles Grayson, 'Lou' Mills and Hugh Topping with their respective crews at Pembroke Dock late in the war when serving with 228 Squadron flying Sunderlands.

Above: Charles Grayson (seated centre) and 'Lou' Mills (standing, far left) with eight other crew colleagues. Navigator Cliff Metcalf, who loaned the original photograph, is on Skipper Grayson's left. *Cliff Metcalf*

Below: Flight Lieutenant Jack Holman and his full crew. Hugh Topping is seated, far right. *Vic Waite*

'Sparks'... Sergeant Peter Scott, wearing his Air Gunner's brevet and wireless operator's 'sparks' badge, before his promotion to Flight Sergeant.
Mary Williams

The aircraft came down at Emlych Farm, on the road to Whitesands Bay. All four crew were killed but it could have been an even greater tragedy.

In its issue of July 13th the *West Wales Guardian* recorded the loss of the four airmen, reporting that the aircraft crashed on a hayguard at Emlych Farm on the Sunday morning.

'The wrecked aeroplane ignited a 15 ton hayrick which set fire to the outbuildings. Livestock was burnt to death and considerable damage was caused to the property. Mr Donald Rees, son of Mr and Mrs H. Rees, had a miraculous escape when he was hurled out of bed when the aeroplane (fuel) tank crashed on the roof, which fortunately did not catch fire. The St Davids NFS (National Fire Service) worked hard to prevent the fire spreading to the dwelling house.'

Local historian David Salmon researched the accident and wrote an article for the *Western Telegraph* in the 50th anniversary year of the accident. It was believed that one engine failed causing the aircraft to swing, he said.

'According to one eyewitness the Liberator had banked low over St Davids and flown along the valley of the (river) Alun in the direction of Emlych. Years later the Rees family of Emlych recalled how the Liberator had torn through a hedgebank and then sliced through a hay pitcher pole,' David Salmon recorded.

'The farmyard was awash with aviation fuel and a pall of oily smoke drifted over the farm and the surrounding countryside.'

It fell to the emergency services and RAF fire crews to remove the unlucky crew and clear away the wreckage, a task which must have taken a considerable time. The flying training among 53 Squadron crews continued but the squadron's ill-starred stay at St Davids was a short one, moving on to Merryfield in September. Crews began trooping flights to India the following month, although by then the Japanese war was over following the dropping of the A-bombs.

The sombre aftermath of the Sunday tragedy came at three graveyards in various parts of the country. At the War Graves section of City Road Cemetery, Haverfordwest, two of the crew, Flight Lieutenant Thomas Hugh Topping and Flying Officer William George Luigi Mills, were buried with full military honours. The bearers to each were six brother officers, a firing party fired a salute at the graveside and the Last Post was sounded. Officiating were Squadron Leader B. Esau, Chaplain of RAF St Davids, and the Rev T. A. Jones, Vicar of Solva, and the CO of the station was represented by Wing Commander Thompson, DSO, DFC.

At Lewes, Sussex, the captain of the aircraft, Flight Lieutenant Charles Grayson, was laid to rest while the funeral of the wireless operator, Flight Sergeant Peter Newton Scott, took place at Sleaford Cemetery, Lincolnshire.

Peter Scott was just 22 and his death was the second wartime tragedy to befall his parents, Reginald and Alice Scott, and the family. Over three years earlier - in May 1942 - another son, Sergeant Donald Keith Newton Scott, failed to return from a Bomber Command mission. He was one of the six-man crew of Wellington X3706 of 156 Squadron which crashed in the northern outskirts of Paris and is buried with his crewmates at Viroflay Cemetery, near Versailles.

Unlike the other three crewmen, Peter Scott had previously served in Iceland with 53 Squadron on long range convoy escort and anti-submarine patrols.

His skipper, Charles Grayson, was aged 32 and a career airman. He had joined the RAF in January 1929 and trained as a metal rigger. In 1935, as the RAF began to rapidly expand, he was accepted for training as an airman pilot and on gaining his wings was posted to No 23 Squadron, a fighter unit operating Demon two-seaters.

In 1937 Charles was posted to the newly reformed No 213 Squadron, operating the single-seater Gloster Gauntlet fighter, and he remained with the squadron into the war years. In January 1939 the squadron converted onto the Hawker Hurricane and it was with the potent Hurricane that 213 went to war.

Like other Fighter Command Hurricane squadrons 213 was pitched into the Battle of France following the German invasion in May 1940 and also flew sorties over the Dunkirk beaches during the evacuation. On May 29th, during a Dunkirk mission,

Unveiling... Mrs Angela Flude, niece of pilot Charles Grayson, unveiled the plaque at Emlych Farm in July 1995, 50 years on from the crash. Also in the picture are the Dean of St Davids, the Very Rev Wyn Evans, Miss Maud Rees, of Emlych Farm, Squadron Leader David Warneford, CO of RAF Brawdy, and Ieuan Griffiths, a founder member of the Pembrokeshire Aviation Group.
Philip Clarke via Angela and Mike Flude

Flight Sergeant Grayson was credited with destroying a Junkers Ju87 dive bomber and with damaging a Heinkel He111 bomber.

In the Battle of Britain that followed 213 Squadron spent several weeks based at Exeter and on August 18th Charles claimed a Messerschmidt Bf110 twin-engined fighter.

Commissioned in June 1941, Charles Grayson went to Canada as a flying instructor, remaining there for over two years. On his return to the UK he opted for a very different role - on flying-boats. After a conversion course onto Sunderlands at No 4 (Coastal) Operational Training Unit at Alness, Scotland, he was posted to No 228 Squadron at Pembroke Dock just after D-Day in June 1944.

Official records show that Charles was posted to 53 Squadron on June 23rd 1945 - just 15 days before he was killed.

Fifty years on the crew members of Liberator KH183 were remembered in a simple ceremony at Emlych Farm, St Davids, in July 1995 where a slate plaque was unveiled on a former milk churn stand. The ceremony was co-ordinated by the Pembrokeshire Aviation Group, in particular by Chairman Tudor Durston, of St Davids, and by David Salmon.

The Dean of St Davids, the Very Rev J. Wyn Evans, dedicated the plaque which was unveiled by Mrs Angela Flude, of Hayscastle, Pembrokeshire, a neice of pilot Charles Grayson.

The plaque was generously made and donated by St Davids stonemason John Williams and among those attending were Mrs Ceinwen Rees and Miss Maud Rees of Emlych Farm and the Commanding Officer of RAF Brawdy, Squadron Leader David Warneford.

Locally, the scars of the accident remained. The wide gap in the hedge, through which the Liberator had careered, could still be made out for many years and the cement grouted roof of the farmhouse showed evidence of the repairs carried out after the damage caused by the fuel tank.

The memorial plaque remains as a simple reminder of a tragedy, close to the cathedral village of St Davids, which occurred so soon after peace had, at last, returned to a battered Europe.

Crew list: Flight Lieutenant Charles Grayson, RAF, Pilot, aged 32, son of Charles Frederick and Ellen Grayson of Lewes, Sussex, and husband of Emily Olive Grayson, of Pembroke

Flight Lieutenant Thomas Hugh Topping, RAFVR, Pilot

Flying Officer William George Luigi Mills, RAF, Flight Engineer, aged 29, son of William Charles and Emma Mills, and husband of Rhoda Mills, of Inverness

Flight Sergeant Peter Newton Scott, RAFVR, Wireless operator, aged 22, son of Reginald and Alice Scott, of North Rauceby, Lincolnshire

* In the Commonweath War Graves records both Grayson and Topping are listed as belonging to 228 Sunderland Squadron although this unit had disbanded in early June. Mills and Scott are correctly listed under 53 Squadron. Hugh Topping's age and family details are not recorded in the War Graves register.

CHAPTER IX

Merlins lead to 'Mossie' tale
de Havilland Mosquito FB6 TE721, June 18th 1947

Coastline... Dale Airfield is located in a very picturesque part of the Pembrokeshire coastline, very close to the magnificent Marloes Sands. It is now in the Pembrokeshire Coast National Park but in wartime there were no landscape constraints on where airfields could be built. Wartime emergency led to many airfields being constructed at scenic locations, and Pembrokeshire has more of these than most. This aerial view probably dates from right at the end of Dale Airfield's active period. *Gill Dashfield*

As an assignment it could not have been better for a young reporter so keenly interested in aircraft and aviation history. The Author - then on the *Western Telegraph's* editorial staff - was dispatched to a field near Solva to find out just what the RAF had turned up at an aircraft crash site.

With photographer Graham Davies in tow I arrived in time to witness the recovery of two Rolls-Royce Merlin engines - one of them in remarkably good condition - and other parts from a marshy corner of the field.

At the time little was known about the circumstances of the crash, or even its date, but it was understood that the Royal Navy pilot had died soon after the accident which involved a de Havilland Mosquito.

The engines were apparently destined for the new Royal Air Force Museum at Hendon and there was

Mossies... Mosquitoes of various marks outside one of Dale's many hangars. Nearest aircraft is Mark VI TE720, coded P7-S, a twin sister to the ill-fated TE721. *Gill Dashfield*

Backdrop... An unidentified Mosquito FB VI against the backdrop of typical wartime architecture at Dale. *Basil Nash*

talk that they would be restored. Sadly, this was not to be the case.

The newspaper cutting about the Mosquito crash at Cerbid Farm, Solva - dated October 1972 - was filed away and I promised myself that one day I would find out more of the story behind the crash.

The two Merlins had powered an example of one of the most famous aircraft in history - the fast, versatile Mosquito, dubbed the 'Wooden Wonder' as it was mostly constructed of wood. Mosquitoes wrote a large and meritorious chapter in the annals of British aviation.

The Royal Navy used Mosquitoes for some years following on the end of World War II and the type became a familiar sight in Pembrokeshire skies as they operated from Royal Naval Air Station Dale.

One of them was TE721, a FB (Fighter Bomber) Mark 6 which had, along with the others, been transferred from RAF service. The Mosquitoes operated with No 790 Squadron, Fleet Air Arm, a second line unit tasked with the training of fighter direction officers who would go on to naval aircraft carriers. Conveniently close to Dale air station, located just south on the Dale peninsula itself, was RNAS Kete *(HMS Harrier)* which was the home of the Fighter Direction School.

TE721 had an eventful year after joining 790 Squadron in July 1946. It was damaged by a bird strike days later and again in a ground handling accident the following November. Just weeks before its final flight the Mosquito had made a precautionary landing after an engine cut.

On Wednesday June 18th 1947 Lieutenant Commander Hamish Muir-Mackenzie, the newly appointed commanding officer of 790 Squadron, taxied TE721 out onto the Dale runway and took off. The Mosquito had two seats but there was no one else on board.

Not long after news was received of an aircraft crash near another of Pembrokeshire's many wartime airfields, at Brawdy, further north. It was indeed the Dale Mosquito.

Official records with the Fleet Air Arm Museum at Yeovilton state that the cause of the accident was 'loss of aileron control after a slow roll, the aircraft crashing while easing out to determine approach speed'. This is substantiated in the highly detailed Air-Britain Historians tome *Fleet Air Arm Fixed Wing Aircraft Since 1946* which records 'loss of aileron control after badly executed roll'.

The *West Wales Guardian*, in a report of the accident, claimed 'It is understood that the undercarriage failed to operate properly'. Further details in the newspaper report recorded that Lieutenant Commander Muir-Mackenzie had died in

Hoisted... RAF Brawdy personnel use muscle power to hoist one of the battered Merlin engines onto a truck in October 1972.
Graham Davies, Western Telegraph

an ambulance taking him to the County Hospital in Haverfordwest. He was 29 and, according to squadron records, had only taken command on June 15th, just three days earlier.

Locally, there were other stories and speculation about the crash. There was a suggestion that the aircraft had had engine problems and had been diverted to Brawdy - then not in use - because it had a longer runway for an emergency landing. And a

Headstone...
Hamish Muir-MacKenzie's Portland Stone headstone at Dale Cemetery. *Author*

story went the rounds that the pilot had been advised to bale out but he had decided to stay with the plane and make a landing.

Whatever really happened the tragic outcome was a crash landing on marshy ground at Cerbid, some two miles from the safely of the Brawdy runway.

Hamish Muir-Mackenzie was brought back to Dale for burial with full military honours. Today his Portland stone Commonwealth War Graves headstone is one of several in the little village cemetery, which has a very impressive war memorial.

The son of Kenneth James and Phyllis Mary Muir-Mackenzie, he is listed in War Graves records as belonging to *HMS Goldcrest*, the shore station name for RNAS Dale. Muir-Mackenzie had a distinguished war record being awarded the Distinguished Service Cross for his involvement in the famous 'Operation Pedestal' convoy to Malta in August 1942. A Lieutenant at the time, he was flying from the fleet carrier *HMS Indomitable*.

The DSC award was listed in the *London Gazette* on November 10th 1942 and he was invested with the medal the following May. Further details of his Fleet Air Arm career are not currently known.

Having witnessed the recovery of the two 1,260 hp Merlins, the Author was interested in what became of them. Some years later he contacted the RAF Museum only to discover that they had no record of them. However, the Author's contacts among the growing aircraft preservation movement firmly suggested that the engines had been sent to a scrapyard, one preservation group later paying several pounds for a part from one of them to help in the restoration of another Merlin.

Today, the engines would be looked upon as 'gold dust' among those who lovingly restore wartime aircraft. Rolls-Royce Merlin engines are highly sought after.

Had the Pembrokeshire Aviation Group existed in 1972 it is possible that an example of the famous Merlin engine would have been rescued for display within the county. The Group has rescued - from scrapyards and elsewhere - many aviation items including propellers which are now on display at Pembroke Dock and at Withybush Airport, Haverfordwest.

CHAPTER X

George Medal for 'Darkie'
Short Sunderland GR V NJ267, March 3rd 1954

The Short Sunderland was in service with the RAF for 21 years, and for nearly all of that time it graced the water and the air at Pembroke Dock. It was here that the mighty Sunderland was pioneered into RAF service, in 1938, and it was here that it finally bowed out of UK operations in 1957.

Happier times... 'Baker' (NJ267) and 'Charlie' (RN288), both of 201 Squadron, formate on a third Sunderland sometime in 1953. Both aircraft were lost in tragic accidents - NJ267 as related here, and RN288 crashed in June 1955 when landing off Eastbourne, where the RAFA Conference was being staged. *Mrs R. M. Willmott*

Over all those years there were very few losses involving Sunderlands within the sheltered waters of the Milford Haven Waterway - less than 20 of the four-engined flying-boats came to grief from all causes, accident and operational. Considering all the aircraft movements which took place at Pembroke Dock in nearly 20 years this was a remarkably small number and testified to the high safety record of the aircraft.

This record was marred in 1954 when a number of accidents involving Pembroke Dock Sunderlands occurred. The worst by far happened on a Wednesday morning when one of PD's big 'boats crashed in the Haven, with the loss of seven of its crew. Even now, more than half a century on, the crash of 'Able-Baker' is still remembered locally.

Wednesday, March 3rd, began as another normal day of RAF activity. Among the Sunderlands carrying out training duties was NJ267, of 201 Squadron. It carried the letter A denoting 201 and the individual letter B. There were 11 crew - more than usual as two 19-year-old airmen were on board for air experience flights.

The crash occurred off Newton Noyes, the *Western Telegraph* recording: 'As the huge aircraft reached its take-off it suddenly dipped and plunged nose forward into the swell. The nose of the machine

Folom... Upside down and forlorn, the remains of NJ267 lie on a Haven mudflat. The rear turret had disappeared from its housing. *John Beckett*

divers, helped for a time by those from the Fisheries Protection flagship, *HMS Coquette*, worked long and hard through the rest of the day and during Thursday to secure hawsers to the hull allowing the wreck finally to be towed into shallow water. There the other six crewmen were recovered but it was some days before the aircraft was finally brought up near the RAF Station. It had been a very long and difficult operation.

As the story behind the accident emerged Pembroke Dock saluted a hero. The flight engineer, 31-year-old Flight Sergeant Ernest Thomas Edward Evans, had escaped quickly from the sinking aircraft but climbed back into it three times to search for crew colleagues.

The *Western Telegraph* takes up the story: 'The first time he saw some hair and found the Navigator, Flying Officer Dalgleish, who had broken an arm. After assisting him out Flight Sergeant Evans returned and seeing more hair floating located Sergeant Jayasinghe who was badly injured. He assisted him out and on to the wing from where a boat rescued him. On his third trip inside Flight Sergeant Evans found no further sign of life'.

This was Pembroke Dock's worst post-war flying accident and had cost the lives of seven airmen.

The following Saturday, in teeming rain, hundreds of local people turned out for the funerals of the pilot and co-pilot, Flight Lieutenants MacLaren and Grinham. They lined the streets between the RAF Station and St John's Parish Church where the service was conducted by the RAF Station Chaplain,

was ripped off and the aircraft filled with water and began to sink immediately'.

The RAF's marine craft section was ever present when flying operations were taking place. A RAF pinnace rushed to the rapidly sinking aircraft, along with a motor boat, the *Tern*, belonging to the Trawler Owners' Association and skippered by Mr Ronald Evans, Milton Crescent, Milford Haven. Between them they rescued five of the crew. One was the aircraft's captain, Flight Lieutenant W. R. MacLaren, but his injuries were so severe that he died soon after.

As the injured were rushed to the RAF Station the mangled Sunderland, almost completely submerged, drifted half a mile towards Pwllcrochan Flats. Part of it reappeared briefly before it settled on its back and disappeared below the waves again. Air Ministry

Squadron Leader R. R. Somervell, and the Vicar, the Rev J. T. Morgan.

Then the procession reformed and marched to Llanion Cemetery where a bugler sounded the Last Post and Reveille and a RAF firing party fired a salute over the graves. Among the many RAF mourners were two of the survivors, Flight Sergeant Evans and Sergeant McIntyre.

The funerals of the other casualties took place at their home towns.

There were commendations at the inquest for Flight Sergeant Evans and Mr Ronald Evans for their rescue efforts. South Pembrokeshire Coroner Mr J. F. Johnson heard graphic accounts from survivors Flight Sergeant Evans, Flying Officer Dalgleish and the wireless operator, Sergeant Gordon Paul McIntyre.

'When the aircraft crashed we went under water and I did not make any attempt to get out as I thought there was no chance at all, but I floated out through the astro hatch. I was fully conscious all the time and it seemed as if I was riding on air. When I surfaced and looked around the aircraft was about 20 yards behind me,' said Sergeant McIntyre.

The other witnesses spoke of the aircraft 'porpoising' as the engines were opened to full power for take off.

'I remember Flight Lieutenant McLaren expressed surprise over the intercom at the amount of swell on the water and he warned us there was likely to be a bumpy take off,' said Flight Sergeant Evans. 'The engines were put at full power right until the time of the crash.'

Medalist... George Medalist Ernest 'Darkie' Evans (centre) pictured at a Coastal Command reunion at RAF Northwood in the early 1960s together with Group Captain W. P. Welch (right), a former Station Commander of RAF Pembroke Dock, and Flight Lieutenant Bill Wing, ex-230 Squadron.
Bill Wing

Boatman Ronald Evans remembered the Sunderland starting to 'porpoise', the nose dipped and he saw the propellers on the port side break into pieces. 'The nose went straight under water and there she remained at an angle of 45 degrees with her tail in the air.'

Another RAF viewpoint came from Squadron Leader R. A. N. McCready, the CO of 201 Squadron. He told the inquest: 'My personal opinion is that the aircraft did not 'porpoise' but I do think it probably pitched across the crest of the steep chop on the water.'

Air Ministry official Mr R. B. A. Cushman read from the report of the inquiry into the accident and went on: 'The court wishes to place on record the fact that Flying Officer Dalgleish and Sergeant Jayasinghe undoubtedly owe their lives to the level headed action of Flight Sergeant Evans who dragged them from the sinking aircraft, and subsequently to the prompt action of Mr Ronald Evans in bringing his boat alongside to effect the rescue.'

The following June there were further headlines with the announcement of the award of the George Medal to Flight Sergeant E. T. E. Evans. At the time of the announcement he was with his squadron on detachment to Malta.

'Darkie' Evans, who joined the RAF in 1938 as a 15-year-old, was later commissioned and attained the rank of Squadron Leader.

The battered remains of NJ267 were recovered following the accident, but the Haven did not give up all of the aircraft. For 40 years 'Baker's' rear turret lay on a mudflat, gradually deteriorating in the seawater and being revealed at very low tides. In the late 1980s the Author was taken across the mudflat by Pembroke Dock D-Day veteran and well known local historian Ted Owens to have a close look at what remained.

Some small pieces were 'rescued' from the turret, along with a piece of perspex which was found nearby. A little further away lay a hatch cover, remarkably intact, and this too was brought to the shore. These pieces were cleaned up and became display items in the RAF Room of the town's Gun Tower Museum.

The turret itself was finally recovered by a Royal Maritime Auxiliary Service vessel in 1993 but its condition was very poor and it was subsequently scrapped.

Crew list: Killed: Flight Lieutenant William Riddock MacLean, RAF, Pilot, aged 33

Flight Lieutenant Norman Frederick Grinham, RAF, Pilot, aged 32

Pilot Officer Henry Charles Watkins, RAF, Navigator, aged 21

Sergeant David Michael Dodge, RAF, Signaller, aged 25

Sergeant Ralph Barraclough, RAF, Flight Engineer, aged 23

Leading Aircraftsman Brian Walter Chadwick, RAF, Wireless operator, aged 19

Leading Aircraftsman Aneurin James Rowlands, RAF, Wireless operator, aged 19

Survived: Flying Officer James Thomas Dalgeish, RAF, Navigator

Sergeant W. S. 'Wally' Jayasinghe, RAF

Flight Sergeant Ernest Thomas Edward Evans

Sergeant Gordon Paul McIntyre

Three more accidents

In 1954 there were three more Sunderland losses from RAF Pembroke Dock. Two involved aircraft from the other resident squadron, No 230, while the other Sunderland belonged to No 201.

The stories behind these losses will feature in another volume in the series.

From the deep... All that was left of the rear turret of NJ267 following recovery by the Pembroke Dock based Royal Maritime Auxiliary Service in March 1993. The Author takes stock! *Author's Collection*

CHAPTER XI

Air day tragedies

Britannia rules... The Britannia emblem can be seen on WL724, another of 727 Squadron's Balliols, which also carries RNAS Brawdy's code letters BY on the fin and 564, the aircraft's individual number at Brawdy. *Via MAP*

Fired up... The Merlin engines of three Balliols are fired up together at Brawdy - a glorious sound. *Fred Dyer*

A highlight of Pembrokeshire summers for nearly 40 years was Brawdy Air Day. Each year on a summer Saturday all of the county's winding roads led to the air station perched very close to the coast near Newgale beach.

Firstly the Fleet Air Arm and then the Royal Air Force put on some exciting shows for the visiting public and the last ever Air Show, in 1991, finally drew the curtain on a memorable sequence of over 30 major events.

In all those years, and with all the air activity over and around Brawdy for the Air Days, there were just two major incidents, both sadly ending in tragedy. Exactly 30 years separated the first accident at an air day from the second.

Boulton-Paul Balliol WL726, August 4th 1956

In its Navy days Royal Naval Air Station Brawdy was known as *HMS Goldcrest*. The station's third annual Air Day was in August 1956 and there was great expectation for the event with over 10,000 people heading for Brawdy.

By tradition Brawdy's Navy air days began with one or more helicopters flying by carrying a welcome for the visitors.

As the *West Wales Guardian* recorded the following week: 'Tragedy stark and sudden hit the Brawdy air display right at the beginning of the programme on Saturday afternoon. Two helicopters carrying huge banners with the words 'Welcome to Brawdy' had hardly completed their circuit of the station when a Sea Balliol, the Royal Navy's latest carrier borne trainer, crashed and burst into flames.

'A gasp of horror went up from the vast crowd as the aircraft, about to pull out of a shallow dive, went straight down and disappeared behind a slight dip at the edge of the airfield, to be followed immediately by black smoke and flames spurting upwards.'

Rescue services rushed to the crash scene near Llandeloy but it was too late to save the pilot, Lieutenant John Mark Mitchell. The 23-year-old, from Liss, in Hampshire, had been giving a display of aerobatics in the Merlin-engined trainer. He was on his second tour of duty at *Goldcrest*.

In the best service traditions the show went on and the crowd's attention was diverted from the crash scene by a thrilling display given in the Navy's latest jet fighter, the Sea Hawk, by Lieutenant Commander D. W. P. Kelly. Named as the Navy's No 1 aerobatic pilot, Kelly's display is particularly remembered for his low level flypast in the inverted position, an eight-point roll and an inverted loop.

A packed flying display, plus many other exhibits, made for a memorable day for all who attended, but sadly the memories of the Balliol crash would long remain for those who witnessed it.

The Sea Balliol was operated by No 727 Squadron which had reformed at Brawdy the previous January as the Dartmouth Cadet Air Training Squadron. Balliols, along with some Sea Vampire jet trainers and a Sea Prince, provided flying experience for junior officers in non-flying roles. The squadron's aircraft were adorned with the head of Britannia, emphasising the connection with what is known as Britannia Royal Naval College at Dartmouth where Naval officers are trained.

Just two days later, on the Monday afternoon, the inquest into Lieutenant Mitchell's death took place. In evidence Naval Commander E. M. Brown said that the pilot had been carrying out an aerobatic manoeuvre. He appeared to misjudge the recovery and the aircraft crashed into the ground and burst into flames.

North Pembrokeshire Coroner Major H. Llywd Williams recorded a verdict of accidental death and expressed sympathy with the relatives.

Heroic efforts by Brawdy personnel to try and save Lieutenant Mitchell were recognised a few weeks later. In a special Order of the Day issued by Home Air Command three 22-year-old Naval airmen were commended for their actions.

The Order of the Day - signed by Vice Admiral C. John, Flag Officer Air - recalled that the three, Leading Airman Gerald Cluett, and Naval Airmen Peter Parker and Donald Bird, had been on duty in a Jeep.

'They set off before the aircraft had actually struck the ground and without waiting for any orders. Driver Cluett drove through two closed gates and over a 3ft high hedgebank. The aircraft was burning fiercely but without cover from any fire fighting appliances Parker and Bird entered the fire, disconnected the oxygen, cut the harness and attempted to extricate the pilot. They discontinued their efforts only when it became obvious that the pilot was beyond their aid. Their protective clothing was badly damaged in the fire. The entire crew showed great initiative and I commend them for their courage and prompt action'.

Brawdy's commanding officer, Captain Frank Stovin-Bradford, DSC, presented illuminated scrolls to the three airmen in recognition of their gallant efforts.

Air-Britain's authoritative reference work, *Fleet Air Arm Fixed Wing Aircraft Since 1946*, gives the official record of the loss of WL726.

'During aerobatics, after a dive and controlled stall turn onto the runway, appeared to complete the manoeuvre with adequate height, but at the last stage mushed into a depression beyond the runway and exploded on impact'.

WL726 was not the first Sea Balliol lost following 727 Squadron's arrival at RNAS Brawdy in 1956. On March 16th sister aircraft, WL727, was forced to ditch off St Davids Head following an engine fire. The pilot, Lieutenant F. Badcock, died but his passenger, Cadet R. G. U. White, although injured, managed to get into a dinghy. He was picked up by a Brawdy helicopter after being sighted by a Sunderland flying-boat.

McDonnell-Douglas RF-4C Phantom, July 24th 1986

Brawdy Air Station returned to Royal Air Force control in 1971 and the tradition of air days was re-established following the arrival of the Tactical Weapons Unit in 1974.

The July 1986 show promised to be as good as any other and a record-breaking crowd of 15,000 flocked to the station. There was a strong United States Air Force element with examples present of the F-111 swing-wing bomber and the F-4 Phantom fighter, two most potent jet types.

The Phantom - a RF-4C version from the 10th Tactical Reconnaissance Wing of the US Air Force stationed at RAF Alconbury, Cambridgeshire - was scheduled in the flying programme. Its crew, pilot Captain Mark Makowski (31) of Wilmington, Delaware, USA, and weapons systems operator Second Lieutenant Dewayne Danielson (24) of Pleasanton, California, USA, lifted the big jet off the Brawdy runway and flew low and fast in front of the crowd line.

Fly by... The USAF Phantom flew slowly by just seconds before it crashed. *Author*

Several people in the crowd, including the Author, noted what appeared to be an object falling from the aircraft and on its next pass the Phantom flew slowly by as if allowing a visual check from the ground.

The Phantom flew out over the coast and disaster followed within seconds. Holidaymakers at Newgale Sands watched in horror as the jet seemed to climb and then fall back into the sea, crashing in the shallows.

One eyewitness looking on from Newgale Hill remembered: 'The Phantom was over the water coming in towards Newgale. It seemed suddenly to have a surge of power, wiggled to the left and then to the right and fell back into the water. It was all over in ten seconds.'

Muffled explosions turned out to be the two crew attempting to eject but they were too low. A Sea King helicopter from Brawdy and other rescue services were quickly on the scene and within an hour the bodies of the crew were recovered from the water. Both parachutes had at least partly deployed.

The Little Haven Inshore Lifeboat and an inflatable from West Wales Divers of Hasguard Cross and their crews provided invaluable assistance off Newgale. Over the following days much of the wreckage was recovered by teams working from the Royal Maritime Auxiliary Service's heavy lift vessel *Garganey*, based at Pembroke Dock. A joint USAF and RAF investigation team was on board the *Garganey* as its crew went about the grim task.

Local sadness and condolences expressed following the accident were especially noted by the US military authorities. Writing to the local press some weeks later Colonel Victor C. Andrews, President of the USAF Mishap Investigation Board, thanked 'the many concerned people who helped with the investigation and also expressed their condolences with the families and friends of the aircrew members.

'We deeply appreciate you sincere concern at the loss of our comrades,' he added.

The findings of the investigations were never officially made known although the *Western Telegraph* later gained access to parts of the report which blamed a low level engine stall for the accident.

CHAPTER XII

Fall of Hawks

Casualties... The three Hawks which were lost 'on active service' from RAF Brawdy.

A lovely air-to-air shot of XX229. *RAF Brawdy 2628G2*

XX197 in 1984, resplendent in the new light grey colour scheme which was adopted for the Hawk fleet. *MAP*

Headlines... A graphic picture of the wreckage of XX197 used by the Western Telegraph to illustrate its headline front page story in May 1988. The red arrowhead insignia of No 79 Squadron - one of the Tactical Weapons Unit's two resident Hawk squadrons - can clearly be seen. *Western Telegraph*

XX192 early on in its Brawdy career, in 1978. Initially it was given the two-tone overall camouflage pattern, as shown here. By the time of its loss it had long been in air defence grey. *MAP B02341*

The last fixed wing aircraft to carry the British roundel from a Pembrokeshire air base was the British Aerospace Hawk. With a lineage stretching back to the pre-World War II days of the elegant Hawker Hart family, the Hawk was a real thoroughbred and today it continues to give sterling service to the RAF.

At RAF Brawdy Hawks served long and well with the Tactical Weapons Unit, training new generations of fast jet pilots in the skills of weaponry and tactics.

Just three Hawks were written off in accidents when flying from Brawdy - a very small number considering the amount of flying training, take offs and landings totalled up by the station's Hawks in 14 years up to 1992.

BAe Hawk TI XX229, July 29th 1983

Hawks entered service at Brawdy in 1978 and in the following few years replaced its famous forebear, the Hawker Hunter. The first Hawk loss was XX229 which crashed into the Irish Sea some 50 miles south west of Brawdy following an engine failure at low level.

Defender... The crest of Royal Air Force Station Brawdy - Pembrokeshire's last military aviation centre. The Welsh motto means 'Defender of the West'. *Author's Collection*

The unnamed pilot ejected safely and was rescued by a Sea King helicopter from Brawdy. Reports vary as to his injuries - from slight facial cuts and a cut to an arm according to one source to back and other injuries, resulting from the ejection, in another.

In a bizarre co-incidence, just half an hour later two Hawks from Brawdy's sister tactical weapons station at Chivenor, Devon, were involved in a mid-air collision near their base. The crew of one ejected immediately while the other crew attempted to return to Chivenor. As the jet was too badly damaged to land the crew flew it out to sea and ejected. All the pilots were soon rescued.

A Milford Haven trawler, the *Picton Sea Eagle*, was chartered by the Ministry of Defence to help search for the Brawdy Hawk and successfully located it in 400 ft of water. By mid August a wing section had been recovered by the RMAS vessel *Garganey* and the trawler had also located the fuselage.

The salvage operation was a prolonged affair, until early November, but neither the engine nor the accident data recorder could be recovered. Evidence available indicated a failure of a compressor blade which damaged the Ardour engine. This, and two other Ardour engine failures, led to new compressor blades being fitted to the Hawk fleet.

BAe Hawk TIA XX197, May 13th 1988

Nearly five years after the first incident, Brawdy's second Hawk loss made major headlines. XX197 suffered engine failure on take off from the station - unluckily on Friday May 13th 1988. At very low level - reports say 150 ft - the two-man crew ejected, their parachutes opened successfully and they landed uninjured on the airfield.

The pilotless Hawk continued on, the *Western Telegraph* reporting that it lost its wings as it clipped a hedge less than a mile from the end of the runway.

'The fuselage came to rest in a field between two unoccupied holiday cottages, its payload of 1,300 kilos of kerosene spewing out and erupting into a ball of orange flame,' the *Telegraph* report dramatically added.

In his book *Lost to Service*, which lists RAF aircraft accidents, Author Colin Cummins says that XX197 was abandoned following engine failure on take off. Its crew, Flight Lieutenant Passfield and Squadron Leader Alan Threadgold, both ejected - Threadgold apparently for the second time in his career.

An inquiry into the incident later blamed a technical fault which had occurred during an engine change.

Bae Hawk TIA, XX192, September 20th 1989

A transit flight to another station turned into disaster when Hawk XX192 plunged into the ground only 500 yards from Brawdy's runway in September 1989. Minutes earlier the trainer had taken off for RAF Scampton, Lincolnshire, only for the pilot to report a fault. When attempting to return to base the jet crashed into a field, with tragic consequences for the two young airmen on board.

The airmen, both just 22, were Flying Officers Alan William George Taylor of Cheltenham and John Patrick Duggan of London. They had been stationed at Brawdy for several months.

Acknowledgements
Special thanks to the following for their help: Deric Brock, Martin Cavaney, Malcolm Cullen, John Donaldson at Aeroplane magazine, Norman Evans, Angela and Mike Flude, Martin Hale, Adrian James, Tony Jenkins, Arthur Jones, Martin Lewis, Roy Lewis, Danny Quinn (for his Foreword and for help over many years), David Smith, Ray Sturtivant (Air-Britain Historians), Ken Williams, Paul Williams and The Western Telegraph. Also fellow members of the Pembrokeshire Aviation Group and all those who have loaned photographs. Grateful thanks also to all at Haven Colourprint for their expertise during the printing schedule.

Also by the Author and Paterchurch Publications
Flying-Boat Haven (Pictorial of RAF Pembroke Dock)
The Sunderland, Flying-Boat Queen, Volume I
The Sunderland, Flying-Boat Queen, Volume II
The Sunderland, Flying-Boat Queen, Volume III
Help From The Heavens (History of 228 Squadron RAF)
Sopwiths to Sunderlands (History of 210 Squadron RAF)
Pembroke Dock Reflections (Pictorial of PD in the 20th century)

FRONT COVER
Liberator. All but one of these young men would be aboard Liberator EV881 when it crashed in the Preseli Hills in September 1944 (See Chapter VII). *George Jared.*

Mosquito. One of the Merlin engines recovered 25 years later from the site near Brawdy where Mosquito TE721 crashed in June 1947 (See Chapter IX). *Author.*

Wellington. The bronze plaque which remembers the crew of Wellington N2749 which crashed at Milford Haven on July 19th 1942 (See Chapter VI). *Author.*

BACK COVER
Ansons. Over the patchwork quilt of rural Pembrokeshire Avro Ansons N9742 (left) and K6285 keep close company for the photographer. Both Ansons were lost when operating from RAF Carew Cheriton in 1940 (See Chapter V). *Royal Netherlands Naval Air Service.*

Bellanca. Residents from the Newport area get a close up view of Bellanca 'Leonardo da Vinci' after its unscheduled arrival on Carn Ingli - the 'Hill of Angels' - in August 1934 (See Chapter II). *Lawswood Collection.*

Ensign. The RAF ensign is folded following the unveiling of the memorial at Emlych Farm, near St Davids, to the crew of Liberator KH153 which came to grief in July 1945. Mrs Angela Flude was assisted by Aviation Group Chairman Tudor Durston (See Chapter VIII). *Philip Clarke via Angela and Mike Flude.*